Rangers and Redcoats
on the Hudson

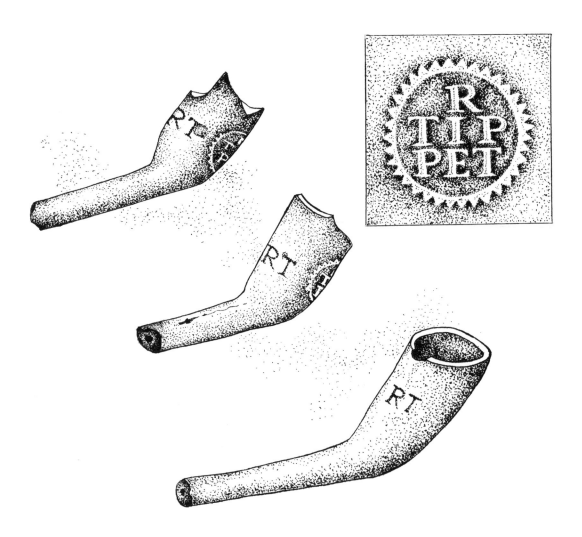

Rangers and Redcoats on the Hudson

Exploring the Past on Rogers Island, the Birthplace of the U.S. Army Rangers

David R. Starbuck

University Press of New England · HANOVER AND LONDON

Published by University Press of New England,
One Court Street, Lebanon, NH 03766
www.upne.com
© 2004 by University Press of New England
Printed in the United States of America

5 4 3 2 1

LIBRARY OF CONGRESS CATALOGING-IN-PUBLICATION DATA
Starbuck, David R.
    Rangers and Redcoats on the Hudson : exploring the past on Rogers Island, the
birthplace of the U.S. Army Rangers / David R. Starbuck.
        p.   cm.
    Includes bibliographical references and index.
    ISBN 1–58465–378–7 (pbk. : alk. paper)
    1. Fort Edward (N.Y. : Town)—Antiquities. 2. Rogers Island (Washington County,
N.Y.)—Antiquities. 3. Excavations (Archaeology)—New York (State)—Fort Edward
(Town) 4. United States—History—French and Indian War, 1755–1763—Antiquities.
5. New York (State)—History—French and Indian War, 1755–1763—Antiquities.
6. Military camps—New York (State)—Rogers Island (Washington County)—
History—18th century. 7. Fort Edward (N.Y. : Town)—History. 8. Rogers Island
(Washington County, N.Y.)—History. I. Title.
    F129.F7S73 2004
    974.7′49—dc22   2004002179

FRONTISPIECE: Examples of "RT" (Robert Tippet) tobacco pipes recovered from
the sutler's site in Fort Edward in 2002. All pipes are drawn at 1:1 except for
the pipe cartouche inset, which is drawn at 1:3. Drawing by Ellen Pawelczak.

Dedicated to the U.S. Army Rangers,

defenders of our nation's freedom.

Contents

Preface

I am indebted to Adirondack Community College (ACC) for its many years of support for this research in the community of Fort Edward. ACC has made it possible for students from many colleges to participate in original research on the French and Indian War, and I am grateful to several staff and administrators for their help over the years. Special thanks must go to President Marshall Bishop, former president Roger Anderson, Vice-President Shelle Kelz, former dean William Gehring, former dean Rosemary Castelli, administrative secretary Nancy Benway, registrar Jeanne Charpentier, and Wesley Winn and Robert Myers of ACC's Media and Publications Office, for their help over the past twelve years.

I also am eager to thank Phyllis Deutsch, my editor at University Press of New England, for her frequent encouragement and for her unfailing support of this volume. Phyllis is every author's dream, an editor who doesn't "nudge" too often but who applies incentives and rewards at just the right times!

When my team began archeological work on Rogers Island in 1991, we really did not know if anything would be left to excavate after the many years of amateur digging on the island. Consequently I am very grateful to all the field and laboratory supervisors, students, volunteers, and professional archeologists who have worked with me, providing the data and many of the interpretations that are contained in this volume. I especially wish to acknowledge Paul Anderson, Ashley Andrews, Joan Baehm, Jon Barber, Carl Barna, Louise Basa, Megan Battey, Craig Brown, Herman Brown, Betsey and Mark Brownell, Frank Bump, Peggy Burbo, the late William Byrd, Cathleen Catalfamo, Debby Campagna, Mary Cassedy, Ann Clay, Deborah Conners, Stephen Coulthart, Ed Dannehy, Joel Dashnaw, Barbara and Gordon De Angelo, Marie Ellsworth, Paul and John Erickson, Jean Etu, John Farrell, Andy Farry, Lachlan Field, Emily Fowler, Linda Fuerderer, Carl Fuller, Karl Gabosh, Donna Gerace, Heather Gilman, Paul Gooding, Chris Haggerman, Elizabeth Hall, Brett Harper, Fred Harris, Phillip Haubner, Bruce Hedin, Janet Henke, William Herrlich, Charles Holcomb, Donna Howard, the late Antonett Howe, Dennis Howe, Dick Ping Hsu, Peggy Huckel, Brad Jarvis, Hans Jensen, Benjamin Kahn, Matthew Kales, Maureen Kennedy, William Ketchum, Jr., Matthew Kierstead, John Kosek, Carl and Margaret Langer, Andrea LaPan, Leah Larcenaire, Cathy Lee, Naton Leslie, Peter Lihatsh, Maria

Liston, Sandra Loach, Kimberly Lovelette, Len Lumsden, Emily Lyons, Sherry Mahady, Ray Matteau, Ken McIver, Phil Mead, Jane Mendocino, Richard Meyer, Gini Miettunen, David Moyer, William Murphy, Joylin Namie, Luke Nikas, Bernard Noble, Mac North, S. Paul Okey, Dorothy, Amy, and Thad Osterhout, Scott Padeni, Merle and Bob Parsons, Fred Patton, the late Joan Patton, Ellen Pawelczak, Ken Rhodes, Marjorie Robbins, Carol Roberts, Victor Rolando, Jene Romeo, Matthew Rozell, Walter Ryan, Frank Schlamp, Bill Selfridge, Royal Sheeley, Roland Smith, Gerd Sommer, Dorothy Stanton, John Strough, Herbert Swift, Judy and Glenn Symon, June Talley, Clarence Thomas, Daniel Thompson, Donald Thompson, Ruth ellyn Thorne, Richard Toman, Janet Truelove, Keith Truesdale, Sarah van Ryckevorsel, Mark VanValkenburg, Virginia Walgren, Alexis Watts, Daniel Weiskotten, Tim Whelan, Linda White, Susan Winchell-Sweeney, Diane Wood, Claudia Young-Palmer, and Janet Zeno.

Some of the veteran workers on our project came back year after year as field supervisors, and these included Matt Rozell, Dennis Howe, the late Antonett Howe, Daniel Weiskotten, William Murphy, Sarah van Ryckevorsel, Cathy Lee, Brad Jarvis, Andy Farry, Marjorie Robbins, Frank Schlamp, and Don Thompson. Barbara De Angelo supervised the field laboratory in 1991, Merle Parsons directed the laboratory from 1992 until 1997, and then Betty Hall in 1998. Merle assembled the artifact counts that form the basis for the bar graph in chapter 1 and tables 7.1 and 7.2, a prodigious task given the many hundreds of pages of artifact catalogs that needed to be reviewed. Sarah Majot and Karl Hemker, Jr., of ARCH TECH then did a superb job of computerizing the artifact data, and Sarah prepared the bar graphs that appear in chapter 1 and the appendixes.

Another major contribution was made by the project's surveyors, Gordon and Barbara De Angelo, who prepared the site maps that appear in this volume. Their joint efforts in the field, assisted by many student helpers, were followed by Gordon's careful drafting of figures 4.1, 4.2, 4.4, 4.5, 4.6, and 8.4. While I have previously published quite a few chapters and articles about this project, it is the new work by Merle, Sarah, Gordon, and Barbara that has been the most critical in completing this, the "final" book about archeology on Rogers Island.

I also owe my thanks to many of the residents of Fort Edward who encouraged our research on Rogers Island over the years, including town supervisor Merrilyn Pulver and town board members Sharon Ruggi, Ed Carpenter, Guy D'Angelico, John Rieger, and the late Bruce Nichols; village mayor Edward Ryan; former supervisors Keith Griffin, Daniel Hayes, the late Loren Sullivan, and Terry Seeley; Fort Edward town and village historian R. Paul McCarty; former Washington County historian Joseph Cutshall-King; Eileen Hannay, manager of the Rogers Island Visitors Center; Neal Orsini, owner of the Anvil Restaurant; and John Weber, a local businessman and village trustee who often stepped forward to help. It is always heartening to have a community's support behind an archeological dig, and the townspeople of Fort Edward were wonderful allies and partners with the archeological team. We especially appreciated the members of the Idle Hour Club, located at the southern end of Rogers Island, who proved to be wonderful neighbors while our excavations were going on.

I am very grateful to Ed O'Dell, of Lake George, New York, who printed nearly all of the photographs in this volume, and Ellen Pawelczak, who drew figures 7.15, 8.8, and the frontispiece.

Finally, I wish to acknowledge the role of William Nikas and Robert Barber, who asked me in 1990 if I would conduct archeology for them on Rogers Island, which they had recently purchased. Their vision of a marina at the southern tip of Rogers Island, with passive walking tours through the historic areas of the island, was the impetus that lured me to Fort Edward to discover whether anything had survived from the military camps created during one of the most fascinating wars in America's history. Their ownership of Rogers Island ended in 1996, and the island passed into other hands, but my gratitude to them continues for their efforts to initiate this research and for the funding they provided in 1991 and 1992. There usually was no compensation for staff in the years that followed, and several of us made very sizable cash contributions to keep the project going. Still, we had research questions we wanted to answer, and collecting information for this book was the reason that we all persevered.

By the time we had completed excavations in 1998, we had dug a large sample of every major category of eighteenth-century military site on the island. So it is that further digging on Rogers Island now, or for some generations to come, would be tantamount to looting. But public interpretation, exhibits, artifact analysis, and further writing should proceed until every possible story has been told about the soldiers and officers who made Rogers Island their home in the late 1750s.

November 2003   D.R.S.

Chronology of Fort Edward and Rogers Island

pre-2000 B.C.	Native Americans begin to hunt and fish on Rogers Island, leaving behind hearths, trash pits, and shell middens scattered along the riverbank. They continue to visit the island until shortly before the first Europeans arrive in the area.
1690	Major General Fitz John Winthrop leads the first recorded military expedition through the "Great Carrying Place" (Fort Edward).
1709	General Francis Nicholson orders Peter Schuyler to build a fort at the Great Carrying Place. The fort is garrisoned with 450 English, Dutch, and Indians equipped with cannons and mortars.
1731	John Henry Lydius builds a trading post at the Great Carrying Place. The trading post is named "Fort Lydius" by the French and Indians.
1755	(September) After the Battle of Lake George, General William Johnson sends General Lyman to build a fort at the Great Carrying Place, and this post is named "Fort Lyman." A month later, William Johnson arrives at Fort Lyman and changes the name to "Fort Edward," in honor of Edward Augustus, Duke of York and Albany.
1755–1756	Barracks, blockhouses, guardhouses, storehouses, and a magazine are completed in Fort Edward in order to counter the French threat in the north. Rogers Island is used by some of the provincial soldiers as a camp.
1757–1758	British barracks, rangers' huts, a blockhouse, and a smallpox hospital are built on Rogers Island.
	(August 10, 1757) The "massacre" at Fort William Henry causes British soldiers to retreat to safety in Fort Edward.

	(July 1758) Major Duncan Campbell of the "Black Watch" dies in a hospital on Rogers Island after General Abercrombie's unsuccessful attack upon Fort Carillon (Ticonderoga).
1759	General Jeffrey Amherst gathers his army in Fort Edward to prepare for an attack upon Forts Carillon and St. Frederic (Crown Point). After the capture of the two forts, the garrison on Rogers Island is greatly reduced.
1763	The Treaty of Paris ends the French and Indian War.
1766	Fort Edward is ordered evacuated, and the stores are moved to the English fort at Crown Point.
1775–1783	A small garrison of American soldiers occupies Rogers Island during the Revolutionary War. They are forced to flee during the approach of General John Burgoyne's army in 1777.
	(July 27, 1777) Jane McCrea is murdered in Fort Edward.
1826	James Fenimore Cooper begins *The Last of the Mohicans* with a description of Fort Edward.
World War I	Soldiers are camped on Rogers Island to protect the railroad.
World War I to present	Rogers Island passes through several hands and is frequently excavated. Earl Stott (the owner from 1960 to 1988) is the principal catalyst for this work.
1964	The Rogers Island Historical Association is created to conduct archeological and historical research into the life and activities of the colonial times associated with Rogers Island, Fort Edward, and the surrounding area.
1991–1995, 1997–1998	Professional archeological excavations are conducted on Rogers Island under the sponsorship of Adirondack Community College and the author.

Rangers and Redcoats
on the Hudson

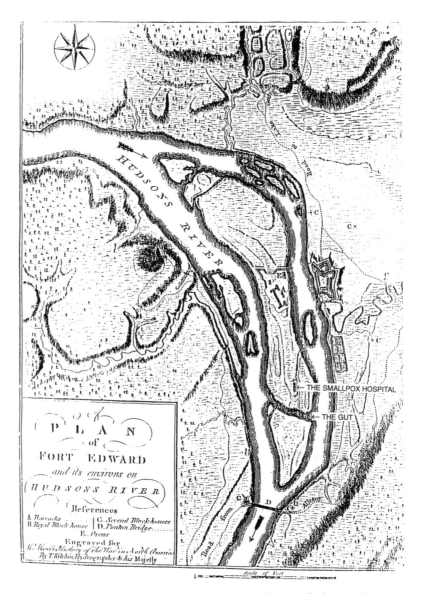

FIG. 1.1. A Plan of Fort Edward and its environs on Hudsons [*sic*] River. Engraved for Thomas Mante, 1772, by T. Kitchen, hydrographer to His Majesty. (Labels "THE SMALLPOX HOSPITAL" and "THE GUT" have been added.) © Copyright The British Museum.

Chapter 1

The Prehistory of Rogers Island

Background

*F*ORT EDWARD is positioned on a natural transportation corridor that permitted Native Americans to travel for hundreds of miles along the Hudson River and through the lakes to the north (fig. 1.1). Still, Native peoples were forced to stop in Fort Edward because of the rapids at Hudson Falls, and the need to portage around the falls earned Fort Edward a very appropriate name, Wahcoloosenchaleva, or the "Great Carrying Place." Local artifact collections suggest that very few Native Americans lived on the upper Hudson River during the Paleo-Indian period (ca. 9500 to 8000 B.C.), just after the glaciers retreated from northern New York State. Few of the distinctively fluted "Clovis" projectile points that were used by the big-game hunters of the Paleo-Indian period have been found locally, and it may be that vegetation and fauna in this area were not rich enough to support a substantial population until the Archaic period that followed (ca. 8000 to 1000 B.C.), when the climate became more modern.

The Archaic was a time of intensive hunting, fishing, and gathering of wild plants by small, nomadic bands, and Native people adapted very successfully to forest and riverine environments. It appears that Archaic camps were often occupied for long periods, and local populations were definitely rising, although it is doubtful that even one hundred people lived in Washington County at any one time. The Early Archaic (ca. 8000 to 6000 B.C.) is represented in Washington County by the styles of projectile points known as LeCroy Bifurcated Base, Hardaway Side-Notched, Kirk Corner-Notched, Kanawha Stemmed, and St. Albans Side-Notched. No intact sites from this period have been excavated locally, and so little is known about the first Native people who traveled along the Hudson River. The same can be said about the Middle Archaic (ca. 6000 to 4000 B.C.), although the distinctive, narrow, stemmed projectile points known in New England as the "Neville" and "Stark" types have been found locally, including the yards of the Fort House Museum in Fort Edward.

While early settlements were no doubt small and seasonal, it was in the Late Archaic (ca. 4000 to 1000 B.C.) that the Native population suddenly grew, and great numbers of Late Archaic artifacts have been found on Rogers Island, at the Little Wood Creek Site (where the Washington County Sewer Authority building now stands), on the property of the Fort House Museum, and at the site of the original Fort Edward. The hundreds of Late Archaic projectile points that reside in local collections include the styles known as Otter Creek, Vosburg, Lamoka, Brewerton, Snook Kill, and Normanskill, but many scrapers, bifacially worked knives, perforators, hammerstones, and worked flakes are also known locally from this period.

Some scholars end the Archaic period with a short "Transitional" period (ca. 1300 to 1000 B.C.), when Native people briefly made stone bowls out of soapstone and fashioned projectile points known as the "Orient Fishtail" type because the base was shaped much like a fish's tail. Soon after, as the first clay pottery, the bow and arrow, horticulture, and a more settled lifestyle arrived in this region, archeologists use the term "Woodland" to describe the next set of adaptations to local resources. Throughout New York State, the Woodland has been divided into the "Early" (ca. 1000 to 200 B.C.), "Middle" (200 B.C. to A.D. 1000), and "Late" (A.D. 1000 to 1500) periods, reflecting changing styles of pottery and projectile points, changing settlement patterns, and new methods of house construction. In the Fort Edward area, there is little evidence for the Early Woodland—typified by the crude, early pottery type known as "Vinette 1"—but the Jack's Reef and Levanna projectile point types are especially common, suggesting that there may have been a large population locally during the Middle and Late Woodland, just before the Mohican people of the early historic period. However, by the time that the first Europeans began arriving on the upper Hudson in the late 1600s, the Native population was largely gone.

Archeological Excavations Conducted at Prehistoric Sites in Fort Edward

Several professional archeological excavations have been conducted at prehistoric sites in the Fort Edward area. One of the most extensive of these occurred at the Little Wood Creek site in the late 1980s, when the Washington County Sewer Authority, Sewer District No. 2, hired a team of archeologists to unearth deeply stratified Indian villages that dated to the Transitional and Late Woodland periods. The three-thousand-year-old Transitional period village was buried eight feet deep, while the shallower Late Woodland occupation contained many storage pits, refuse pits, hearths, much decorated pottery, and pits containing thousands of freshwater clamshells (fig. 1.2). Six prehistoric skeletons were also uncovered here that were

FIG. 1.2. A Late Woodland pit feature on Little Wood Creek, filled with thousands of freshwater clamshells taken from the Hudson River. Courtesy of the Rogers Island Visitors Center.

turned over to the Onondaga Nation for reburial nearby. The project was directed by Joel Grossman, and the Little Wood Creek site revealed important evidence for early agriculture and long-distance trade, demonstrating that Fort Edward was long an important center of Native American settlement (see the box "Excavations at the Little Wood Creek Site").

In the 1990s, many prehistoric artifacts were also found in the yards of the Fort House Museum in Fort Edward, which is one of the oldest standing houses in Washington County. During excavations that I directed there between 1993 and 1995, I recovered thousands of chert and quartz flakes, a stone gouge, scores of projectile points—including Otter Creek, Stark, and Brewerton points—but very little prehistoric pottery (figs. 1.3 and 1.4). The

FIG. 1.3. Otter Creek projectile points (*left*) and a stone gouge (*right*). The point on the lower left and the gouge were both excavated by the author from the grounds of the Fort House Museum, while the point on the upper left was found about 50 years ago on the grounds of Fort Edward High School. Both of the projectile points were manufactured of chert.

★ Excavations at the Little Wood Creek Site

What may be Fort Edward's richest prehistoric site lies in the Little Wood Creek area on the east bank of the Hudson River, just south of the ruins of the original Fort Edward. During the construction of a modern sewage treatment plant in the 1980s, a comprehensive study of this site was ordered by the Washington County Sewer District. The extensive archeological dig that followed was directed by Joel Grossman, now of Grossman and Associates in New York City, and he found evidence for two major prehistoric settlements. Federal funding made it possible to conduct this large rescue excavation prior to the construction of the treatment plant.

Grossman's team discovered storage pits, refuse pits, and hearths from the Late Woodland period (ca. A.D. 1000 to 1300), underlain by a Transitional period village (ca. 1000 B.C.). The Transitional village dated to the Frost Island phase and was represented by an intact living floor that contained more than eighty thousand artifacts. There were five major hearth areas, and the distribution of artifacts suggests that both men and women lived on this site, where they hunted, cooked, and made use of the river.

The artifacts from the Little Wood Creek site are being curated at the Rogers Island Visitors Center, where the more diagnostic lithic tools include many examples of Lamoka, Susquehanna

Broad, and Levanna projectile points from the Late Archaic, Transitional, and Woodland periods, as well as assorted bifaces, scrapers, and net sinkers. Most are made of chert taken from various New York State quarry sites, although a few were fashioned from quartzite. Perhaps the very best artifacts discovered at Little Wood Creek are the sherds of prehistoric pottery, including hundreds of decorated rims and shoulders dating from the Late Woodland period. A total of 3,059 prehistoric sherds were found, either in surface excavations or in the many basin-like storage pits and trash pits that were dug. The sherds came from a minimum of 34 different pottery vessels, and there are at least four distinct tobacco pipes.

Archeologists use a variety of attributes to classify sherds into types, including how the surface was treated (whether smoothed, polished, cordmarked, etc.), how the decoration was done (whether incised, fingernail impressed, punctated or stamped), the size, type of temper, and the diameter of the rim. Using these attributes, the vessel types identified at the Little Wood Creek site included the types known as Kelso Corded Collar, Bainbridge Collared Incised, Owasco Corded Collar, Oak Hill Collared, Chance Incised, Castle Creek Incised Neck, Sackett Corded, Owasco Horizontal, Owasco Platted, Otstungo Notched, Bainbridge Notched Lip, and Pseudo Scallop Shell. Of course, these archeological terms would have meant little to the Native Americans of the Late Woodland, but they enable archeologists to make cultural comparisons with other prehistoric sites.

The Little Wood Creek site, a general view looking north of Deep Cut A. This shows the excavation of Late Archaic living surfaces, ca. 1500 B.C. Courtesy of the Rogers Island Visitors Center.

FIG. I.4. Examples of projectile points excavated from the yards of the Fort House Museum, all from Pit 14 on the south side of the Fort House. *Left to right:* a Stark point of shale, an untyped, side-notched point of quartzite, an Otter Creek point of chert, and an unfinished point of chert.

FIG. I.5. Projectile points excavated in 2002 at the original site of Fort Edward.

Fort House is located further back from the Hudson River than the Little Wood Creek site, so it was significant that the yards of the Fort House contained artifacts that were generally older.

Ironically, the excavations conducted by Adirondack Community College in 1995, 1996, 2002, and 2003 at the original site of Fort Edward revealed one of the richest prehistoric sites of all. The modern yards and houses that cover the fort on the east bank of the Hudson River were found to overlie dozens of Late Archaic and Woodland projectile points (fig. 1.5), scrapers, perforators, pottery sherds, and thousands of flakes of chert, evidence of prehistoric workshops located on the terrace above the river. Until recently, the most exciting prehistoric discovery made at the fort site was a ground stone ax excavated by Daniel Weiskotten in 1995, but in the summer of

FIG. 1.6. A soapstone pot fragment of the Frost Island phase, found in 2002 just south of the sutler's site.

FIG. 1.7. Evidence of burning, with charcoal and ash, inside one of the prehistoric middens (Site 2) on Rogers Island. All scales are marked in 10-cm units, and the scale arrow always points north.

2002 we also recovered two small fragments from a "Micmac" stone tobacco pipe.

Just south of Little Wood Creek, on the edge of the sutler's site we excavated in 2001–2002 (see chapter 8), we found a fragment from a soapstone bowl (fig. 1.6), apparently an extension of the Transitional period village that was discovered by Joel Grossman in the 1980s. On reflection, it is fascinating that so much evidence for Native occupations can still be present after many years of modern settlement and disturbance.

The Prehistory of Rogers Island

The years of excavation on Rogers Island have certainly focused upon the military sites from the French and Indian War, but much of the island is covered with small campsites from the Late Archaic, Transitional, Middle Woodland, and Late Woodland periods. From the 1960s through the 1980s some of these sites were excavated by members of the Rogers Island Historical Association, but that organization focused almost exclusively upon the island's military occupation—it reported very little about the island's prehistory.

More recently, the excavations by Adirondack Community College have revealed numerous prehistoric firepits and trash pits (figs. 1.7 and 1.8), projectile points (fig. 1.9), butchered deer bones, pottery, tobacco pipes (fig. 1.10), and shell middens (food dumps that contain shellfish). The clearest

FIG. 1.8. Prehistoric and historic features at Site 1, facing south. A prehistoric firepit is visible at the lower left, and it contained pottery, deer bones, and fire-cracked rocks. The prehistoric trash pit at the upper left contained butchered deer bones. The trash pit at the lower right was from the eighteenth-century military occupation and contained cow bones and an iron fish hook.

FIG. 1.9. Projectile points and a drill from various locations on Rogers Island. *Left to right:* a Bare Island point of rhyolite, a Levanna point of chert, a Levanna point of quartzite, a Wading River point of quartz, a chert drill on a reworked Snook Kill base. *Bottom:* a Snook Kill point.

FIG. 1.10. Clay tobacco pipe bowl fragments from the prehistoric middens at Site 2 and Site 14 on Rogers Island.

evidence for a prehistoric settlement, and not just a dump, was found at Site 1, underlying the military storehouse built there in the 1750s (see fig. 5.1). We exposed a number of Late Woodland pit features at that site, and our testing suggests that that camp or village could have been much larger. Other prehistoric sites on Rogers Island do not appear to be quite as rich, but thousands of chert flakes, smaller numbers of quartz and quartzite flakes, pottery sherds, and occasional projectile points, drills, scrapers, and bifaces are scattered across the island (see the graph "Total Numbers of Native American Artifacts").

In 1991 we found a very extensive shell midden alongside the road that runs to the southern tip of Rogers Island, and this contained many thousands of freshwater clamshells, hundreds of pottery sherds (chiefly of the Oak Hill phase of the Late Woodland period), and occasional projectile points. It would appear that these shells had been thrown along the riverbank during Archaic and Woodland times, and the subsequent deposition of silt along the east side of the island has moved the shell midden at least a hundred feet inland.

In 1992 we discovered an exceptionally large firepit or "roasting platform" (fig. 1.11) just north of the remains of a storehouse in our Site 1 area (see fig. 5.1). One of our students, Charles Holcomb, spent ten days exca-

Total Numbers of Native American Artifacts

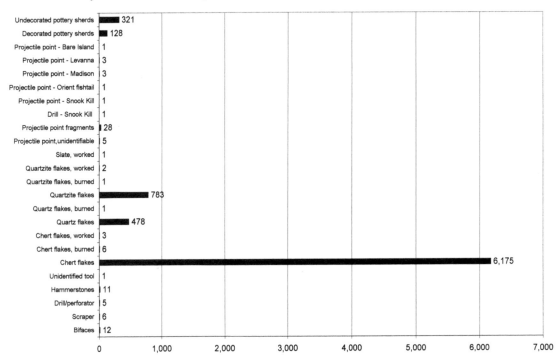

FIG. 1.11. A "roasting plat-
form" being excavated at
Site 1, N51W16, in 1992.
Facing southeast.

vating this great concentration of fire-cracked rocks. It was absolutely
packed with thousands of fragments of butchered and burned deer bones
and chert flakes, as well as lesser numbers of quartzite flakes and pottery
sherds. The ceramics were identified by the late Dr. Robert Funk as Late
Woodland, from circa A.D. 1350. The pattern of charcoal and ash off to the
side of the firepit suggested that the fire had been built on a platform of
river rocks, and then the fire and charcoal were raked to a depression on the
east of the platform so that the rocks could be used for roasting meat. This
interpretation is based on the absence of a charcoal layer over the stones
and the absence of artifacts among the stones, coupled with the wealth of
artifacts found in the charcoal on the east.

Perhaps our most unusual prehistoric discovery on Rogers Island was
made in 1993 in Trench 2 (Site 11) when a charcoal-stained firepit was discovered at N134W53 that contained a set of crossed deer antlers just 20 to
30 cm deep, overlain by a few undecorated body sherds (figs. 1.12 and 1.13).
A deer mandible was present in the pit, a chunk of fire-cracked rock lay
atop the antlers, and we found some bird bones and claws just underneath

★ The Discovery of a Prehistoric Grave in 1991

While archeologists working in the United States today generally do not seek to discover prehistoric graves, sometimes we do find them by accident. During our first season on Rogers Island, in 1991, we decided to test along the bottom of an old bulldozer trench that had been dug by looters on the west side of the modern dirt road that runs to the southern tip of Rogers Island. Almost immediately, we encountered human teeth and bone fragments that caused us to stop. Unsure as to whether they represented the remains of an eighteenth-century soldier or a much earlier Native American, we sent some of the teeth to the New York State Police Forensics Identification Center in Albany. When we were informed that their odontologist, Lowell Levine, was away working on a forensics case in Hawaii and would not be back for a few weeks, we decided to await his return and avoided the burial site altogether.

When Dr. Levine subsequently visited us in Fort Edward, he identified the remains as those of a Native American based on the presence of shovel-shaped incisors, a distinctively Native and Asian trait. We of course asked how we should proceed and were told to remove the skeleton and send it to Albany for analysis. I next asked Dick Ping Hsu, then the regional archeologist for the North Atlantic Region of the National Park Service, if he would like to personally conduct the excavation, and he went to work. The shallow burial was in a flexed position, with the arms and legs drawn up tightly against the body, and there were no associated artifacts that would help us to assign the skeleton to a time period or a culture. It lay within a very few centimeters of the ground surface, where it could not be protected from collectors, and it was also in a very fragile, decayed condition.

Midway through the study, we were visited by a film crew from Channel 13 in Albany, and they began filming our diggers as they worked else-where on the island. I deliberately kept them away from the area where Dick was doing his excavation, until finally they hit me with the question, "What's going on over there?" I suppose I could have lied, but instead I told the reporter that it was something he could not film. Unfortunately, this thoroughly whetted his appetite, but I finally elicited a promise that the footage would never be used on the air, and we allowed the filming to proceed. What a mistake!

On the following day, a Friday, I received a phone call informing me that "the public has a right to know!" and that "someone else might release the story first!" I was then notified that the exhumation would appear on the evening news that night at 6:00 p.m. After a helpless "but, but . . . ," I realized that a difficult situation was about to become much worse. As I made phone calls to New York State officials and to Native Americans, trying to keep everyone informed, it was clear that finding a prehistoric skeleton was the worst thing we could have done. What followed were months of negotiations for the disposition of the remains, hotel and meal bills for visiting Native elders, and flights to the Onondaga Reservation in Syracuse before the reinterment finally occurred several months later at a secret site elsewhere on Rogers Island.

Along the way, just about everything that could have gone wrong did, including a front-page story in the *Glens Falls Post-Star* titled "Indian Skull Found on Rogers Island." Juxtaposed next to this heading was a cartoon of a head, taken from a separate story, showing how beachgoers in Florida had been burying themselves in the sand with only their heads showing. The proximity of the two stories was bizarre and, unfortunately, tasteless and offensive. Members of the Native American community were not pleased.

Almost from the beginning, we gave up all

rights to analysis, we refused to show the bones to anyone who was not Native American, and we did no further excavations in that part of the island. In hindsight, I believe that everything we did was respectful to the remains of this unknown man or woman, but I do not wish ever to go through such a complicated, expensive, and political process again. And ironically, at the end, the religious service performed over the remains was a modern Onondaga service. Because the skeleton was most likely that of a Mohican, or at least an ancestor to the Mohicans of the historic period, the service may well have been performed by traditional enemies of the deceased. This made me feel uncomfortable at the time, and it still does.

FIG. 1.12. Deer antlers buried at the bottom of a prehistoric firepit at Site 11, N134W53.

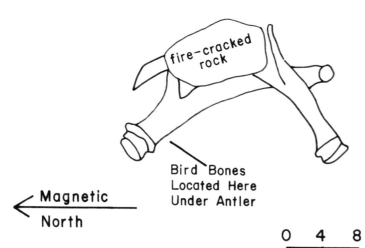

FIG. 1.13. A drawing of the deer antlers inside the firepit in fig. 1.12.

fire-cracked rock

Bird Bones Located Here Under Antler

Magnetic North

0   4   8 cm.

the antlers. In the absence of datable artifacts, we cannot assign a definite age to this feature, but the presence of the prehistoric sherds indicates that this firepit dates to at least the Woodland period.

Our team also discovered a Native American burial in 1991 that we turned over to the Onondaga Nation for reburial (see the box "The Discovery of a Prehistoric Grave in 1991"). While we do not know whether other prehistoric burials occurred on Rogers Island, that possibility seems very likely because of the ease with which grave shafts could have been dug into the sandy soil.

While archeologists have excavated relatively few prehistoric Indian sites in Fort Edward, every one of them has been extremely rich in artifacts, suggesting that there is tremendous potential for future Native American research along this stretch of the Hudson River. The sides of the Hudson and the islands in the river provided Native people with a rich food supply, and Fort Edward's location just south of a major falls in the river ensured that all early travelers had to get out of their canoes and portage. These factors suggest that there may well be dozens of other short-term Archaic and Woodland campsites in Fort Edward that are still waiting to be discovered by future generations of archeologists.

Chapter 2

The History of Rogers Island
During the French and Indian War

RITISH COLONIAL STRATEGY in the eighteenth century permitted Fort Edward, New York, to become one of the most important military bases in the New World. While the fort that was given the name "Fort Edward" came somewhat later, there were earlier fortifications in that community, beginning with "Fort Nicholson," built under the command of Colonel Francis Nicholson during the 1709 conflict known as "Queen Anne's War." Fort Nicholson was garrisoned by 450 men, including seven companies of "regulars in scarlet uniform from old England." A crude stockade was built at that time to protect storehouses and log huts.

John Henry Lydius, a Dutch fur trader from Albany, arrived at the site of Fort Nicholson in 1731 and constructed a trading post from which he traded with Indians over many years. Lydius claimed this land under a title granted to the Reverend Dellius of Albany in 1696. According to a 1732 French map, the trading post may have been surrounded by storehouses and was fortified, so it is sometimes referred to as "Fort Lydius." Lydius may also have built a sawmill on Rogers Island. It is unknown whether the Lydius trading post was destroyed in 1745 as French and Indian raids were conducted along the Hudson River, but some of the buildings were apparently standing when Fort Edward was constructed nearby in the 1750s. Modern historians disagree about the exact siting of the trading post, with some placing Lydius's log house within the perimeter of the later fort and others placing it farther south.

Construction of Fort Edward began in August of 1755, just before the Battle of Lake George was fought that September some twelve miles to the north. British General William Johnson had ordered engineer Captain William Eyre to lay out the log fort, as well as Fort William Henry, in what is now the village of Lake George. These two forts became the first well-built British forts in North America, and both were imposing, bastioned fortifications of the type designed by a renowned French builder of forts, Sebastien Le Prestre Vauban (1632–1717).

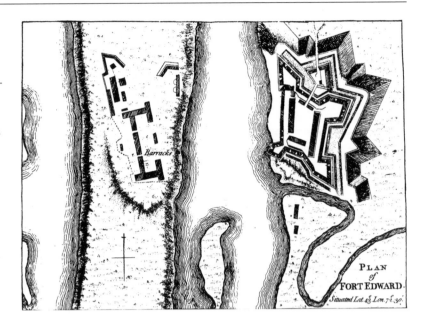

FIG. 2.1. Plan of Fort Edward and Rogers Island published ca. 1763. The barracks buildings on Rogers Island appear on the left, and Fort Edward stands on the right, on the east bank of the Hudson River. The stream at the lower right is Little Wood Creek. The two small buildings south of the creek may be sutlers' storehouses, although they may pertain to the brewery constructed there in 1759. Courtesy of the National Archives of Canada.

Fort Edward was initially named "Fort Lyman," after Johnson's second-in-command, Major General Phineas Lyman, who arrived there in August of 1755. However, just a month later, William Johnson changed the name to "Fort Edward" to honor Edward Augustus, the Duke of York. The new fort was constructed on the east bank of the Hudson River, at or near Lydius's trading post, and Fort Edward was a much more substantial fortification than Fort William Henry. Fort Edward was situated so as to help protect the portage route between the Hudson River and Lake George, and it was surrounded by a moat and earth embankments that were topped with pickets. On the inside it contained an East Barracks and a West Barracks, along with sheds, casemates, a guardhouse, a hospital, a powder magazine, and a blacksmith shop. British regulars lived within the fort and also along the extensive, fortified lines that ran north and east from the fort, along what is now Route 4 in Fort Edward. However, the fort itself was but the centerpiece in a giant military encampment that included Rogers Island in the Hudson River, a bridge from the fort over to the island, gardens, and a total of eight blockhouses (fig. 2.1). One of the blockhouses, termed the "Royal Blockhouse," is now sited in the modern town of Moreau and was one of the two largest blockhouses in North America. An extensive tent camp was raised on Rogers Island during the latter part of 1755.

Provincial soldiers and rangers traveled to Fort Edward from the colonies of New Hampshire, Massachusetts, Rhode Island, Connecticut, New Jersey, and New York, and at least twenty-seven different regiments were represented among the provincials and British regulars. The Scottish Highland regiments included the 42nd (Black Watch), 45th, 51st, and 77th, and some of the other units stationed in Fort Edward were the 48th Regiment of Foot, the 55th Regiment of Foot, Connecticut Provincial Rangers, and the 27th, 44th, 46th, 60th, and 80th Regiments.

In order to provide provisions to the soldiers, sutlers or merchants also settled in Fort Edward, and there are contemporary historical references to both a "Mr. Best" and a "Mr. Pommery," who provisioned the troops. "Mr. Best" apparently built his home and a storehouse just south of the fort in 1757. On approximately this same site, General Amherst ordered the construction of a brewery for spruce beer in 1759.

Over the space of several summers, the population at this military base seasonally swelled to as many as fifteen thousand or sixteen thousand, making Fort Edward and Rogers Island the principal British military base in the colony of New York and one of the largest cities in the American colonies. At the end of each season, British regulars returned to Albany for the winter, whereas provincials returned to their homes. This typically left only a small garrison in Fort Edward during the winter months. Throughout its period of use, the base in Fort Edward was clearly critical to the war effort as the largest hospital complex, supply depot, and training camp of that time. No major battles ever occurred in Fort Edward, and it is unfortunate that great encampments do not seem to generate the same excitement as battle sites. However, there was one raid on July 23, 1757, when a French force under Joseph Marin de la Malgue attacked the outworks of Fort Edward.

The distinguished military units that saw service in Fort Edward included Major Robert Rogers and his Rangers, who camped in small log huts on Rogers Island for about two and a half years between 1756 and 1759 (fig. 2.2). "Rogers' Rangers" became an independent unit on March 23, 1756, when Rogers was commissioned a captain by William Johnson. From a modest beginning with just sixty privates, three sergeants, one lieutenant, and an ensign, Rogers' Rangers eventually grew into a force of about four hundred. Men such as Thomas Speakman and Humphrey Hobbs led companies of Rangers under Rogers's command, and Major Rogers also relied upon units of Stockbridge (Mohican) Indians. While the island had previously been known by a variety of names, on September 11, 1758, the name "Rogers' Island" first appeared in the *New-York Mercury*, reflecting how closely the island had become associated with Major Rogers (see the box "Major Robert Rogers and His Rangers"). In that November, the *London Chronical* described a Ranger raid and was datelined "Rogers Island." Still, in spite of all the emphasis given to Rogers' Rangers, it must be remembered that they were but one out of the many units stationed in Fort Edward. From an archeological perspective, that means most of the artifacts and features found today on Rogers Island were left behind by provincials, regulars, or other ranger units.

FIG. 2.2. Robert Rogers. A colored plate by Helene Loescher. Courtesy of the Fort Edward Historical Association.

★ Major Robert Rogers and His Rangers

The most daring of the British colonial forces were the rangers, frontiersmen who fought using tactics adopted from the Indians. These rugged early Americans fought the French and Indians throughout the forests of northern New York, New England, and southern Canada. A ranger's uniform typically consisted of a green outer coat, waistcoat, shirt, and linen or canvas drawers; brown leggings; moccasins; and a flat Scottish bonnet. Equipped with tomahawk, sheath knife, musket, cartridge box, powder horn, bayonet, haversack, and bedroll, a ranger was prepared to spend weeks on scouting duty, pursuing and ambushing his enemies before reporting back to the British Command.

Between 1757 and 1759, Rogers Island in Fort Edward was the main base camp for "His Majesty's Independent Companies of Rangers" and especially for Rogers' Rangers. This was the elite fighting force named after Major Robert Rogers, the dashing frontiersman who had been born in Massachusetts in 1731 to Scottish parents. The name "Rogers Island" was already being used in British newspapers in the 1750s, suggesting that Rogers and his men had achieved a nearly instant celebrity. Rogers' Rangers lived on the island in huts, and from there they scouted enemy movements and made raids upon Ticonderoga and other French and Indian settlements, notably in 1759 at the Abenaki village of St. Francis (Odanak) on the St. Francis River in Quebec, Canada. Their other most famous engagement was the so-called Battle on Snowshoes, fought just west of Ticonderoga on March 13, 1758, at which time Rogers led about 180 men against a superior force of French and Indians.

It was on Rogers Island that Rogers wrote down a series of "Ranging Rules" in 1757, instructing his men in the principles of forest warfare. While British and French regulars stood in orderly rows, firing their muskets in volleys, Rogers advocated guerrilla tactics that were much better suited to the American frontier. In a very real sense the Rangers were the forerunners of modern Special Forces units, and their tactics for fighting in the woods have been adopted by irregular fighting forces all over the world. Today these rules have been summarized in the *Ranger Handbook* of the United States Army as follows:

Standing Orders, Rogers' Rangers

Rangers were organized in 1756 by Major Robert Rogers, a native of New Hampshire, who recruited nine companies of American colonists to fight for the British during the French and Indian War. Ranger techniques and methods were an inherent characteristic of the frontiersmen in the colonies, but Major Rogers was the first to capitalize on them and incorporate them into a permanently organized fighting force. His "Standing Orders" were written in the year 1759. Even though they are over 200 years old, they apply just as well to Ranger operations conducted on today's battlefield as they did to the operations conducted by Rogers and his men.

1. Don't forget nothing.
2. Have your musket clean as a whistle, hatchet scoured, sixty rounds powder and ball, and be ready to march at a minute's warning.
3. When you're on the march, act the way you would if you was sneaking up on a deer. See the enemy first.
4. Tell the truth about what you see and what you do. There is a Army depending on us for correct information. You can lie all you please when you tell other folks about the Rangers, but don't never lie to a Ranger or officer.
5. Don't never take a chance you don't have to.
6. When you're on the march we march single file, far enough apart so no one shot can't go through two men.
7. If we strike on soft ground, we spread out abreast, so it's hard to track us.

Battle on Snowshoes 1758.
Painted by J. L. G. Ferris.
Courtesy of Chapman Historical
Museum.

8. When we march, we keep moving till dark, so as to give the enemy the least possible chance at us.

9. When we camp, half the party stays awake while the other half sleeps.

10. If we take prisoners, we keep 'em separate till we have had time to examine them, so they can't cook up a story between 'em.

11. Don't ever march home the same way. Take a different route so you won't be ambushed.

12. No matter whether we travel in big parties or little ones, each party has to keep a scout twenty yards ahead, twenty yards on each flank and twenty yards in the rear, so the main body can't be surprised and wiped out.

13. Every night you'll be told where to meet if surrounded by a superior force.

14. Don't sit down to eat without posting sentries.

15. Don't sleep beyond dawn. Dawn's when the French and Indians attack.

16. Don't cross a river by a regular ford.

17. If somebody's trailing you, make a circle, come back onto your tracks, and ambush the folks that aim to ambush you.

18. Don't stand up when the enemy's coming against you. Kneel down, lie down, hide behind a tree.

19. Let the enemy come till he's almost close enough to touch. Then let him have it and jump out and finish him up with your hatchet.

Rogers himself was colorful and controversial, and even today he is revered by some as a brave and charismatic leader, while challenged by others as given to exaggeration and self-promotion. There is no denying that before he began his military service, Rogers had been accused of passing counterfeit money; later, large numbers of his men were killed while on campaigns; and still later, he led a Tory regiment against patriot forces during the American Revolution. All the same, whether we choose to view him as a hero or a rascal, everyone acknowledges the effectiveness of Rogers' tactics. This is exemplified today by the number of soldiers who read and respect his writings and by the number of Native Americans who still abhor his memory.

Rogers spent several years in debtors' prison in England before returning to North America at the start of the American Revolution. He became a lieutenant colonel of a battalion of Queen's Rangers, but when the Revolution went against him, Rogers returned to England in 1782. He spent more time in debtors' prison and developed a drinking problem. His life continued in relative obscurity, and Rogers died in London on May 18, 1795, where he is believed to have been buried in a pauper's grave.

Perhaps the strangest twist on the Rogers story

came in 2000, when individuals from Fort Edward and Long Island used dowsing to try to discover Rogers' grave in a small cemetery in Dunbarton, New Hampshire. Their plan was to dig him up and transport him to Fort Edward for reburial as a tourist attraction. This was followed in 2002 by the use of ground-penetrating radar in the same cemetery. It seems that they hadn't been able to exhume Rogers from his actual grave on the grounds of St. Mary's Church in Newington, England, so they had decided it would be easier to get permission to exhume him from a New Hampshire cemetery where some of Rogers' relatives were buried! Appropriately, a Merrimack County Probate Court judge and the trustees of the Dunbarton Cemetery decided they wanted no part of this and denied a request to drill holes into the cemetery. In spite of such silliness, Rogers' legacy is very powerful even today for both Special Forces and reenactors, and he has been the subject of many scholarly and popular works, including the book and movie *Northwest Passage*. The popular movie by that name was released in 1940 and starred Spencer Tracy as Major Rogers and Robert Young as one of his Rangers. It is undeniable that Rogers has been "rediscovered" by each passing generation, and the adulation for this frontier woodsman is currently stronger than ever.

In August of 1757 Fort Edward was commanded by General Daniel Webb, and thus it figured prominently in the siege and so-called massacre of the British garrison at Fort William Henry, described in James Fenimore Cooper's novel *The Last of the Mohicans*. Fort Edward was the fort from which Hawkeye and his companions journeyed to Fort William Henry, and it was the site to which many British and provincial soldiers returned after the surrender of the Fort William Henry garrison to French general Louis Montcalm. Fort Edward thus figures at the center of one of the greatest controversies of the French and Indian War, because many Americans have believed that General Webb should have done more to relieve the soldiers at Fort William Henry when they came under attack.

Within the Fort Edward encampment, Rogers Island rose to prominence as the seasonal home of great numbers of soldiers and officers between 1756 and 1759, with construction peaking during 1757 and 1758. This troop buildup coincided with General Abercrombie's disastrous campaign against the French and their leader, the Marquis de Montcalm. Fort Edward was the staging area for Abercrombie's army in 1758 before they departed to attack the French breastworks at Fort Carillon (Ticonderoga). After that battle, the wounded British and provincial troops then returned to the hospitals on Rogers Island that had been set up for their treatment.

During this period, British soldiers lived within massive barracks buildings on Rogers Island and within the fort, each perhaps as much as three hundred feet long, whereas provincial soldiers, rangers, and some officers lived in rows of small huts, houses, or tents (see the box "Excerpts from the Diary of an Ordinary Soldier"). Historical records indicate that other structures and features on Rogers Island included a large or "Great Block-house" in the center of the island (this was later turned into a hospital), a large storehouse for provisions, a smallpox hospital at the south end of the island, a sawpit, and small privies or "necessary houses" located along both riverbanks. Extensive gardens were planted, both on the island and on the east bank of the Hudson River, that provided fresh vegetables for the soldiers and officers.

In addition to the smallpox hospital, built in late 1757, there were general-purpose hospital rooms scattered throughout barracks buildings on the island and inside the fort. Easily the best-known officer to have died in a hospital on Rogers Island was Major Duncan Campbell of the Forty-second Highland Regiment, who had suffered a mortal wound during Abercrombie's attack upon Fort Ticonderoga on July 8, 1758. Campbell later achieved fame in a Robert Louis Stevenson ghost story, published in *Scribner's Magazine* in 1887. In this gothic tale, Campbell was still at his family castle of Inverawe in Scotland when he was forewarned of his fate by the ghost of Donald, his murdered cousin: "Farewell, till we meet at Ticonderoga." On July 9, 1758, the ghostly apparition fulfilled its pledge as Campbell lay mortally wounded outside the walls of Fort Ticonderoga. The Highland officer was one of the many casualties from Ticonderoga to be carried to the hospital complex at Fort Edward. Campbell died nine days later and is now buried in Union Cemetery in Fort Edward.

Abercrombie's defeat in 1758 was followed by a new British campaign in 1759, led by General Jeffrey Amherst. Fort Edward was again used as a staging area by the British, and this time their siege of Fort Ticonderoga was successful. Some of Amherst's wounded soldiers were sent back to a hospital on Rogers Island for treatment. The subsequent establishment of a more northerly base at Crown Point made Fort Edward increasingly unnecessary—it was no longer the front line of defense against the French—and Fort Edward was reduced to essentially a base for supplies and hospitals. Fort Edward was garrisoned at a reduced level until April of 1766, when it was ordered evacuated and the stores moved to His Majesty's Fort at Crown Point.

Many scholars have pointed out that during the ten-year-period when British forces were based in Fort Edward, a very sizable number of soldiers and rangers were trained who went on to become prominent commanders during the American Revolution. Among the residents of Rogers Island were Major General John Stark, who led American forces at the Battle of Bennington; Major General Israel Putnam, of Bunker Hill fame; Brigadier General Benedict Arnold; Major General Philip Schuyler; William Franklin, son of Benjamin Franklin; Paul Revere; and Noah Grant, the great-great-grandfather of President Ulysses S. Grant. Given the size of

★ Excerpts from the Diary of an Ordinary Soldier, Jabez Fitch, Jr.

Jabez Fitch, Jr. (1737–1812), of Norwich, Connecticut, served in Fort Edward during campaigns in 1756, 1757, and 1758. A prolific writer, he recorded daily events in his diary throughout most of his life, and he prepared some of his best entries while stationed on Rogers Island. This included the period when Fort William Henry was attacked and surrendered to the French and Indians, at which time Fitch was just twenty years old and a sergeant. Some colorful samples of his writing follow:

June 10, 1757: About 11 oClok we were Alarmd By A Smart Firing over where ye Carpenters was at work We Not Having our Arms with Us made ye Best of our way into ye Fort   Then I Got My arms and Toock [took] out where ye Party was Attacted there found Some Dead Men But ye Enimy were Drawn of & Genll Lyman Persuing them with a Party &c   4 Men were brought in and Buried after about 2 Hours . . . The Men that were Kild [killed] Were all Scalpt   Some of Them their Brains Run out   Wilm Mortawomocks Brest was Cut open & His Hart Torn out — Our Men that are Mising We Can't Tell whether they are Dead or Captivated [captured]

July 15, 1757: at Noon they Gave Me a Vary Good Dinner among other Varietyies a Fig Pudden [pudding]   in ye Afternoon there was Several Showers — this Day there was a Genll Revue of ye Women in ye Army to Examen Whether they Had the &c or Not [a reference to inspecting camp followers for disease].

July 23, 1757: Just as ye Troop Beet to Relieve ye Guard We Was Alarmd By A Smart Fireing in ye Woods where our Carpenters were at work — The Firing Lasted Near ½ an Hour   as Soon as Possable Genll Lyman Got orders to Go out with a Party But there was a Larg Number went out Before — I went with ye Genll But Before we Got to ye Party

the armies in Fort Edward in the 1750s, there may well be several million Americans today with ancestors who resided on Rogers Island or in the vicinity of Fort Edward.

During the time of the American Revolution, Fort Edward once again saw many troop movements, but the fort was finally abandoned for good in the 1780s, and the modern village grew up over the ruins of the fort. Property owners have long found remnants of the fort, typically timbers and bricks, in their cellars along Edward, Old Fort, and Moon Streets. Rogers Island fared somewhat differently because its southern half was not built upon, and it has seen very little activity of any sort since the colonial wars. The sites of barracks buildings, huts, tents, storehouses, kilns, and hospitals are amazingly well preserved, and Rogers Island now survives as one of the most pristine sites of the French and Indian War.

Attacted ye Enimy were Drawn off & Carryd off their Dead if they Lost any as was Sopsd [supposed] they Did — We all Returnd in again in about an Hour & Brought in our Dead & wounded Men [This was the only assault ever made upon Fort Edward. The French under Joseph Marin de la Malgue attacked the outworks of the fort, and about a dozen men were killed.]

August 25, 1757: in ye Afternoon I Bought 7 Plums for a Copper   This Night Robert Jaquais of Capt Gallups Company was Whipt [whipped] 120 Lashes for Unfaithfullness on His Post & Samll Chapman of Capt Wellss Company was Whipt 50 for ye Same Crime &c.   Then I went on ye Piqt [picket]

September 5, 1757: At 8 oClok Corpll Dorman & Luallen Rice were Shot For Desertion — I was Not at this Execution By Reason of Being on ye Piqt [picket] But I Was Informd By Some that were Present that Dorman Died a Profest [professed] Roman Catherlick [Catholic] — & Rice A Protestant &c.

September 15, 1757: In ye Morning I Went Down to ye Brook in ye Swamp & Had a Genll Wash of all my Linen.

October 18, 1757: At Night We Drinked three Quarts of Cherry Rhum at our tent

January 3, 1758: In ye Morning ye River was So High that it Ran into Many of their Hutts & Drove them out   Capt: Durke was Drove out &c   Som of their Hutts were Waist Deep in Water ye River Being So High   This was also a Stormy Day & Vary Slippery Every thing Being Covered with Ise . . . Som of our Men yt [that] were Drounded out of their Hutts Came & Lodged with Us

February 3, 1758: This Morning we Had a Vary Diverting Sight of Druming a Woman out of ye Garrison which Made Us Much Laugh &c

Source: *The Diary of Jabez Fitch, Jr., in the French and Indian War, 1757*

Many of Fitch's written comments deal with very ordinary, day to day activities, but as the above entries suggest, this monotony was broken by the occasional enemy raid, by executions, by whippings, by the river rising and drowning soldiers in their tents, and by disciplinary actions involving camp followers. We love to say that a typical soldier's life was probably rather boring, yet Fitch was a careful observer of camp life who enjoyed his meals and his rum, who was exposed to death almost daily, and who spent his active hours on picket duty and on construction details.

Chapter 3

Rogers Island from the 1760s to 1990: The Fascination Begins

*W*ITH THE CLOSE of the French and Indian War, the buildings on Rogers Island were abandoned, but we do not know whether they were taken down, rotted in place, or were burned. After the Treaty of Paris in 1763, settlers began moving into the area, including Hugh Monro, one of the Highlanders of the Seventy-seventh Regiment of Foot, which had been disbanded in the Fort Edward area. Monro received a land grant to Rogers Island from George III on August 5, 1766, and he thus became the first private individual to own the island.

During the American Revolution, a small garrison of American soldiers occupied Rogers Island between 1775 and 1777. The island again became a staging area for soldiers, but it does not appear that any significant new buildings were constructed at that time. General Burgoyne's British and German army captured the island and Fort Edward at the end of July in 1777, while en route to Saratoga, but the town was subsequently retaken by American forces on October 10 of that year. The island probably ceased to be used by the military in about 1781, and the Committee on Safety in Albany ordered any remaining fortifications to be razed in 1789.

After the war, Hugh Monro sold Rogers Island, which was used for farming in the years that followed. A Charles Rogers bought the island in 1821, the Champlain Canal was dug just east of the island in the 1820s, and the first railroad tracks were laid out across the island in 1847. The nineteenth-century historian Benson Lossing, writing in *The Pictorial Field-Book of the Revolution* in 1851, became one of the first scholars to recognize the archeological potential of the island: "Almost every year the plow turns up some curious relics of the past upon the island, such as bayonets, tomahawks, buttons, bullets, cannon-balls, coin, arrow-heads, &c."

During the Civil War, the New York Volunteers conducted drills on Rogers Island. Shortly after, the island was purchased by a Ralph Freeman in 1866, and it was renamed "Freeman's Island." Later, the island was sold in 1876 to a George Bradley, and the name was changed to "Bradley's Island."

FIG. 3.1. Aerial view of Rogers Island and the adjacent east bank of the Hudson River (north is at the top). The railroad tracks that cross Rogers Island appear at the upper left; a narrow triangle of land owned by New York State appears at the upper right edge of the island; and the property owned by the Idle Hour Club is in the lower left corner of the island. The rest of the island (south of the railroad tracks) is owned by Mr. Frank Nastasi. Courtesy of the office of Real Property, Washington County, New York, and the New York State Office of Cyber Security and Critical Infrastructure Coordination, Albany, New York.

The next owner was a George Mead, who in 1908 sold part of the southern end of the island to the Idle Hour Club, a private men's club, which built a clubhouse there. The adjoining Hudson River channel was subsequently dredged by New York State between 1909 and 1918, and the dredgings were placed on top of the former barracks sites to a depth of ten feet and more. On a positive note, the dredged spoils finally gave a measure of protection to the archeological sites that lay underneath. This thick, heavy silt and clay is still filled with sherds of Fort Edward stoneware as well as fragments of timbers that were dredged from the river bottom.

There was yet another brief flurry of military activity during World War I, when soldiers were stationed on Rogers Island to protect local railroad bridges. This was followed by significant alterations to the island in 1917 when the channel or "gut" between the main island and a smaller island to the south was filled in, just north of the site of the Idle Hour Club. As a result, the current shape of Rogers Island is rather different from its appearance on British military maps of the 1750s (fig. 3.1). The only activity here during World War II was the operation of a barge-making company at the southern end of the island.

The Early Years of Digging: 1960–1988

It was after the sale of the historic parts of Rogers Island to Earl Stott in 1960 that large-scale digging began, and huge areas were excavated on the southern forty acres of the island (see the box "Remembering Earl Stott"). A great deal had survived from the French and Indian War because there had been little or no construction on the island during the American Revolution, and frequent flooding by the Hudson River helped to bury the foundations of early buildings under sand. After 1960, bulldozers removed trees and surface layers of dirt to get down to 1750s levels, and volunteers with hand tools flocked to the island to dig. Typically digs were on weekends, and participants were expected to bring their own tools. Few excavation records were kept during this period, and the artifacts were neither conserved nor properly curated. Many different groups assisted in the excavations, including the Auringer-Seelye Chapter of the New York State Archaeological Association; they were one of the few groups that did keep records, which were turned over to Earl. Also, in 1973, Janice and Robert Henke, then graduate students in anthropology at SUNY Buffalo, directed part of the digging (fig. 3.2).

For everyone who participated during this period, there was one main requirement, that they turn over all of the artifacts they discovered to the island's owner. Earl's fervent wish was to eventually reconstruct the former military buildings as a tourist attraction, or at least to create a credible museum on Rogers Island. Within a few years, Earl joined with friends to form the Rogers Island Historical Association, which saw itself as a "history-minded group interested in Rogers Rangers and the French and

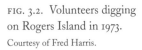
FIG. 3.2. Volunteers digging on Rogers Island in 1973. Courtesy of Fred Harris.

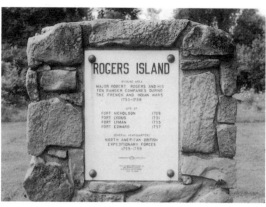

FIG. 3.3. The monument and flagpoles erected on Rogers Island by Earl Stott in 1964. Courtesy of Fred Harris.

FIG. 3.4. The monument erected on Rogers Island in 1964, honoring Rogers' Rangers and the various forts that were constructed in Fort Edward. Courtesy of Fred Harris.

Indian War. It is a non-profit organization dedicated to the preservation and study of objects and events concerning Colonial and Revolutionary periods associated with this Island and the surrounding area."

In 1964 Earl and his son erected a monument on Rogers Island to honor the memory of Robert Rogers and his Rangers (figs. 3.3 and 3.4). A very positive step forward was taken on July 24, 1973, when forty acres of Rogers Island (including the land owned by the Idle Hour Club) were listed on the National Register of Historic Places, recognizing the significant history and integrity of the island.

The years of digging by Stott and the Rogers Island Historical Association resulted in the discovery of many fireplaces—most with a standardized 24-inch-wide hearth—many hut sites, and possibly some barracks buildings. Most features, especially fireplaces, were removed as collectors dug underneath, searching for artifacts, but no adequate maps have survived to show where these were. Excavation pits were rarely measured out, dirt was never sifted, and many pits were never filled in. Still, an impressive array of artifacts was recovered, including hundreds of coins (minted in England and Spain), musket balls, gunflints, tobacco pipe fragments, pottery sherds, wine bottles, British army uniform buttons, and animal bones. Less common were bone-handled knives and forks, pewter spoons, ice creepers, fish hooks, trade axes, several nearly complete plates of porcelain and delft, four Brown Bess muskets, part of the wood from a cannon carriage, cannonballs, and a brass pocket sundial compass (manufactured in Germany between 1730 and 1740). Just after the island was sold in 1988, three canteens were also taken from a backhoe trench (figs. 3.5 and 3.6).

★ Remembering Earl Stott, the Longtime Owner of Rogers Island

In 1960 the southern half of Rogers Island was purchased by Earl Stott, who wanted to save the island from being developed into an industrial complex. After growing up in the vicinity of Fort Ticonderoga, Earl had become a tool-and-die maker for General Electric and lived in Hudson Falls, New York. Earl especially appreciated the Scottish Highlanders in the British army who had lived and fought locally, and the documented presence of five Highland regiments in the Fort Edward area perhaps guaranteed that Earl would want to "own a piece of history!"

In the years that followed, Earl and his friends exposed large areas of Rogers Island, explored underneath many of the dredge piles, excavated the fireplaces within many huts and possible barracks, and unearthed thousands of artifacts. Earl did keep some general notes on his digging, although not the detailed records that are prepared by archeologists. He loved to speculate about whom each artifact had actually belonged to, and he had a curious habit of identifying almost everything he found as an officer's prized possession. During the years of digging, Earl started a host of small businesses on the island, and he sold shares in a marina (which never came to fruition), laid out a golf course, and even built quite a few Liberty Poles at the time of the nation's bicentennial.

One of the largest of Earl's projects was held on a weekend in 1961 when hundreds of Boy Scouts came to help him dig. Many of these former scouts still live in the local area and are now in their fifties, and several have told me about the excitement of their discoveries that weekend. I can almost identify with this event because, at a class reunion some years ago, one of my old friends in the Boy Scouts told me that he "remembered" my having been there digging next to him; he reminisced about exposing a brick and then looking over to see what I might be finding. But honestly, I wasn't there!

In an amusing bit of irony, in 1991 I was being interviewed on Rogers Island by Steve Scoville of Channel 13 News in Albany when Steve suddenly gave me a funny look and exclaimed, "My gosh,

A group digging on Rogers Island in 1973. Courtesy of Fred Harris.

I remember this place—I dug here with my Boy Scout troop years ago!" Steve had been one of the many diggers thirty years before, and it was not until we were in the middle of our interview that he suddenly remembered his one-time archeological adventure with Earl.

As far as I can remember, it was not until 1986 that I first met Earl, at the end of a talk I delivered at Saratoga National Historical Park. On that occasion, Earl poured dozens of Spanish and British coins into my hand, my jaw probably dropped, and he definitely got my attention! While I truly wish that Earl had never done any digging and that he had left Rogers Island completely intact for future generations of archeologists, at the same time I cannot deny that his charisma and charm "turned on" great numbers of people to local history and archeology. Earl never lacked for enthusiasm, and he was undeniably the finest storyteller to ever live in Fort Edward.

On a personal note, I once had dinner with Earl and his family in the house that he had built himself at the southern tip of Rogers Island. Earl was a most gracious host, and as we spoke, artifacts were passed around the dinner table, his sons played with cannonballs on the sofa, and Earl's love of history was obvious and intense. When Earl spoke, you never quite knew which stories to believe, but he could talk for hours about the Rangers, the Scottish Highlanders, his excavations, his artifacts, and his great plans for the future of Rogers Island.

I hope the work that has occurred on Rogers Island since Earl's passing would have pleased him, because Earl always stated that he wanted "Ph.D.s" and universities digging on his island. I believe he would have liked the exhibits in the Rogers Island Visitors Center, and he definitely would have enjoyed the renewed interest by reenactors, townspeople, and scholars in everything that happens on Rogers Island. In a very real sense, we are all continuing his legacy.

Among many unusual finds, one of the most distinctive was a brick that bore the date "1759." Other bricks bore impressions of deer feet.

The Rogers Island Historical Association published a small volume on some of its findings, *Exploring Rogers Island*, and it also reprinted the extremely informative diary of one of the Rangers who had lived on the island, *The Diary of Jabez Fitch, Jr., in the French and Indian War, 1757*. However, while undertaking many commendable activities, members of the association dug extensively into sites around the perimeter of the barracks complex, in areas where it was believed that soldiers' huts and tents had formerly stood. Some of this digging was reported in local newspapers, although a survey of available articles reveals so many inconsistencies and divergences from the known historical record that newspaper and magazine accounts are more confusing than helpful. And detailed archeological reports simply were never written or published.

Exploring Rogers Island is the only systematic account of the early findings on the island, yet it contains no archeological drawings or maps showing what was found and where. Also, the artifacts that are pictured or described are no longer in the community of Fort Edward, so it is not

FIG. 3.5. A canteen discovered in a backhoe trench on Rogers Island in 1988. This was conserved by Nancy Demetteneyre of the New York State Office of Parks, Recreation and Historic Preservation.

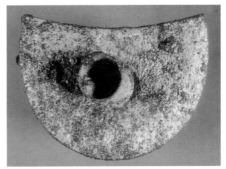

FIG. 3.6. An end view of the canteen pictured in fig. 3.5.

possible to verify many of the artifact identifications. Still, it may safely be said that Earl believed he had located the site of the "Great Blockhouse" on the island, complete with many associated medical artifacts that reflected the later use of the site as a hospital; the foundation from an armorer or smith's shop; two rows of huts "running the length of the island"; the site of "a regimental tailor's shop"; more than a dozen fireplaces in one area and "about twenty fireplaces" in the barracks area; and hard-packed earth from living floors in many different parts of the island. Clearly Earl and the Rogers Island Historical Association made some very major discoveries.

During the many years of digging, some fascinating and fanciful stories were created about Rogers Island, some of which really do stretch the truth. One account claimed that the base of a whipping post had been discovered, surrounded by human finger bones, although there is no surviving evidence that the post was a "whipping post," nor that the bones were human. It was claimed that a fourteenth-century Jesuit "altar vase" had been discovered, which the discoverer claimed he had "carbon-dated," an unusual claim since carbon 14 dating cannot date pottery or porcelain. What was claimed to be a Native American "trophy skull" was found underneath the floor of a hut. This was given to a lawyer in the nearby community of Saratoga Springs, who displayed it in a box on his desk. A variation upon this story held that this was actually the skull of Ranger Carty Gillman, who had turned king's evidence against Major Rogers and so was murdered by his fellow Rangers. It was also claimed that human amputation pits had been found, even though other diggers have told me that these were usually trash pits containing butchered animal bones. And in perhaps the most bizarre tall tale of them all, it was claimed that the reason for the French and Indian War was that gold, silver, and copper had been found in upstate New York, and that British officers—engaged in an early "gold rush"—were actually smelting gold and silver on Rogers Island. It was even claimed that gold bars had been found on Rogers Island!

Twenty-eight years of theories and yarns were interspersed with tales about Rogers' Rangers and the equally glamorous Scottish Highlanders. Toward the end of this period, there was even an article that appeared in 1988 in a real estate magazine, *Yankee Homes*, offering Rogers Island for sale for $400,000 and stating, "perhaps untold finds await the curious shovels of the new owners," adding "you can go dig up your own collection when you buy the island." Rogers Island was no longer a valued military site that everyone wanted to protect; instead, it was evolving into a collectors' paradise where digging up artifacts was the only real objective.

The unfortunate result of these activities was that Rogers Island developed a reputation among historical archeologists and preservationists of being the most disturbed, the most overdug, and the most compromised major site of the French and Indian War, capable of damaging the reputation of any professional archeologist who might consider working there. At the same time, many non-archeologists believed that this "archeology" was all very exciting. Ironically, after all the digging that had been done, perhaps half of the local residents whom I questioned believed that there must be artifacts everywhere on the island because so many diggers had already been successful. The other half believed that nothing could possibly be left! The many years of fantasies and myths had created a body of folklore in which nothing was real, nothing adequately documented; and every child and adult in the region who had an interest in history had had the opportunity to participate in the excitement. Also, inevitably, there were claims that "professional archeologists" had been involved and "state archeological experts have said . . . ," yet these experts were never named. It was all very confusing.

Still, there was a widespread awareness that something needed to be done to save Rogers Island, and in 1987 the Fort Edward Village Board attempted, unsuccessfully, to raise the money to buy the island and turn it into a historical park and museum. When that effort failed, it became almost inevitable that the island would soon be sold to developers.

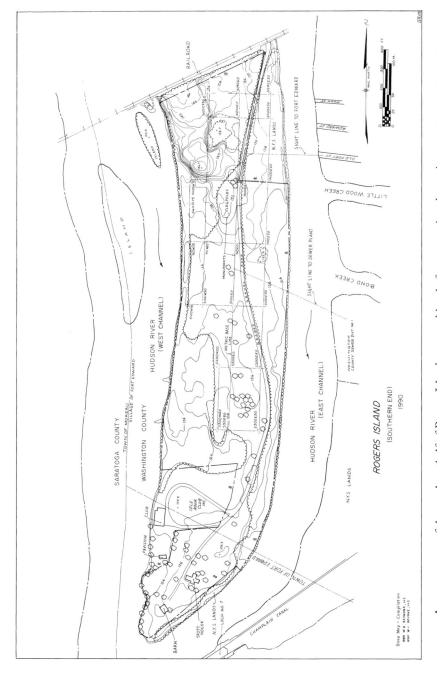

FIG. 4.1. A contour map of the southern half of Rogers Island, prepared just before excavations began in 1991. Courtesy of Gordon De Angelo.

Chapter 4

Modern Archeology on Rogers Island in the 1990s

B Y THE LATE 1980s, professional archeologists and New York State officials were increasingly concerned that Rogers Island had nothing left to offer, that almost thirty years of digging had produced a hodgepodge of stories but almost no usable information. It was unknown, except by word of mouth, where sites had been discovered, and no one knew whether any information of historical value could still be gleaned from the island if new work were to be initiated.

Fortunately, this gloomy prospect began to change in 1988 when two local businessmen, Robert Barber and William Nikas, purchased the southern portion of Rogers Island in order to construct a private marina and health club close to where Stott's house stood (fig. 4.1). They were not initially aware of the historical significance of the island but quickly came to realize that history might be a strong draw for boaters along the river and for those who might buy shares of stock in their proposed development.

Initially there was little reason to believe that developers would be kind to Rogers Island, but instead of delivering the coup de grâce, Nikas and Barber soon barred further access to collectors and made the decision to construct their marina buildings only in disturbed areas at the southern tip of the island where there had been no eighteenth-century occupation. They further decided to create an open-air cultural park around the archeological sites and to prohibit any construction atop the military encampment.

They next approached me, and I agreed to be the professional archeologist who would oversee a long-term research program on Rogers Island. This began with a small Phase IA/IB survey in the spring of 1991, as mandated by New York State law, that would ensure new construction did not impact archeological sites (fig. 4.2). Nikas and Barber's proposal for marina construction required the developers to avoid, or mitigate, adverse effects upon cultural resources at the southern end of the island where regrading and the construction of utility lines and access roads were due to occur. While they were under no legal obligation to inventory the remaining,

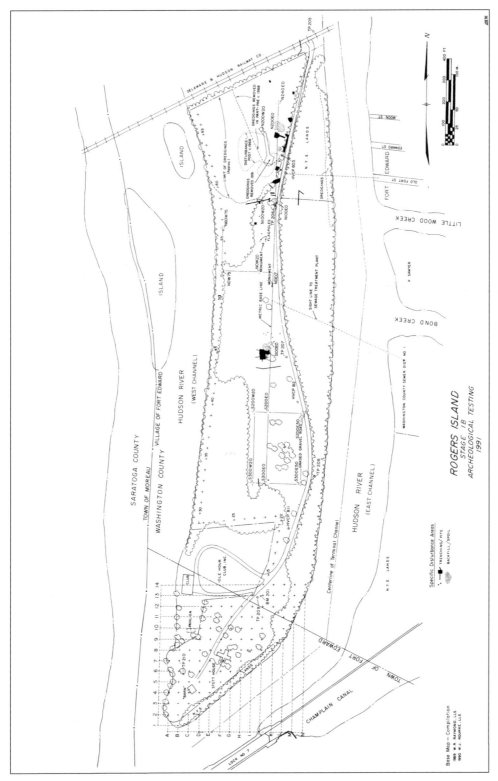

FIG. 4.2. A base map of the southern half of Rogers Island, showing the Phase 1B archeological testing that was performed in early 1991. This also shows the coordinates of the master grid that was superimposed over the island that year; all subsequent testing (figs. 4.4–4.6) was conducted according to that grid. Courtesy of Gordon De Angelo.

FIG. 4.3. The initial testing at Site 1 in 1991, just north of the flagpoles and monument erected by Earl Stott. Facing south.

more historic portions of Rogers Island, the new owners nevertheless supported my plans for annual summer excavations that would use volunteers and college classes. We then approached Adirondack Community College, which agreed to provide course credit for students. As the discussions proceeded, community leaders, historians, and others were gradually drawn into the planning process, and this helped the community of Fort Edward feel more responsible for the future management and protection of Rogers Island.

We held our first field season on Rogers Island in 1991 (fig. 4.3), and we continued during the summers of 1992, 1993, and 1994, always for six weeks at a time. We then halted excavations when Nikas and Barber decided to put the island up for sale, although we briefly reopened the site of a barracks fireplace in 1995, to permit filming by The Learning Channel. We subsequently returned in 1997 and 1998 under the auspices of a new property owner.

Each summer we used crews of sixty to seventy professionals, students, and experienced volunteers, with each participant working under professional supervision for a minimum of two weeks. Some sites we tested very lightly, whereas others we dug more intensively to identify all the architectural elements within the footprint of a given building. Table 4.1 lists, and figures 4.4, 4.5, and 4.6 depict, all the areas excavated on Rogers Island over that eight-year period. We often enlisted a tour guide who led visitors to sites on the island, and several thousand visitors were presented with information about the history of Fort Edward and Rogers Island.

Most visitors received a tour of the excavation areas and information

Table 4.1

Sites Excavated on Rogers Island, 1991–1998

Site*	Description	Excavation years
1	Storehouse; latrine; prehistoric site	1991, 1992, 1993
2	Dwelling 1; midden	1991, 1993, 1994
3	Barracks area; Dwelling 6	1991
6	Midden on west edge of island	1991, 1993
7	Stott "Great Blockhouse"	1991
11	Dwelling 2; Trench 2 through barracks area	1992, 1993, 1994, 1995
12	Trench 1 through barracks area	1992
13	Roadside, disturbed hearth area	1992
14	Smallpox hospital; prehistoric site	1991, 1992, 1993, 1994
15	Looters' backdirt pile	1992
16	Trench 3 through barracks area	1992
17	Roadside, midden area (same as Site 2)	1992
18	Midden	1997, 1998
19	Dwelling 3; Dwelling 4; Dwelling 5	1997, 1998

*Sites 4, 5, 8, 9, and 10 were either not excavated or contained no artifacts.

about archeological field techniques, and they were given stern warnings about how excavations must *only* be done under the supervision of trained professionals, emphasizing that collecting is unacceptable. Our efforts to further public education included printing and distributing information booklets, developing exhibits to place in local public institutions, and giving slide lectures to just about every local church, Lion's Club, Rotary Club, or school class willing to listen.

1991 Research

Our work each year featured different sites and different priorities, but certainly no later year equaled 1991 for sheer richness of finds and unexpected surprises. In that first year we discovered a pattern of post molds that outlined a possible storehouse (Site 1), and we found that firepits and trash pits from a prehistoric settlement underlay this same building. We dug most of a dirt-floored tent that I am referring to here as "Dwelling 1," and this contained the remains of two brick fireplaces and traces of wood from temporary walls around the perimeter. Next to this tent, we dug an extensive shell midden that contained thousands of freshwater clamshells and modest numbers of prehistoric pottery sherds and projectile points (Site 2) (fig. 4.7). We next brought in power equipment and used it to trench through the dredge atop the former barracks area and then dug by hand underneath

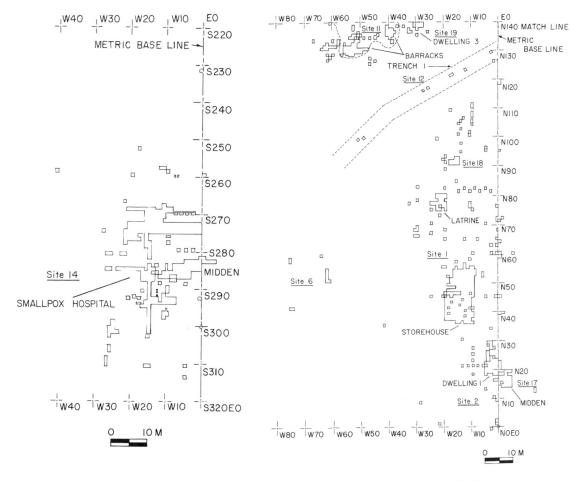

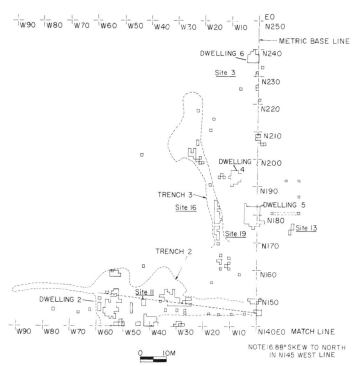

FIG. 4.4 *(above left)*. Figures 4.4–4.6 depict all the sites that were excavated between 1991 and 1998. Figure 4.4 shows the southern end of Rogers Island, between s320– and s220–; this area features the site of the smallpox hospital (Site 14). Courtesy of Gordon De Angelo.

FIG. 4.5 *(above right)*. Figure 4.5 begins 220 meters north of fig. 4.4 and includes all excavation sites between N0– and N140–. This is perhaps the richest part of Rogers Island and includes Dwellings 1 and 3, the barracks area (Sites 11 and 19), and the storehouse and latrine areas (Site 1). Courtesy of Gordon De Angelo.

FIG. 4.6 *(left)*. Figure 4.6 depicts all of our more northerly excavations, between N140– and N250–. This includes Dwellings 2, 4, 5, and 6, as well as the northern end of the barracks area. These are the areas that were buried most deeply under dredge from the Hudson River. Courtesy of Gordon De Angelo.

the dredge (Site 3) (fig. 4.8). We also excavated at the south end of Rogers Island in an effort to find traces of the smallpox hospital (Site 14), and we sifted backdirt in the area where Earl Stott once believed the island's "Great Blockhouse" had been located (Site 7). We even made many small, relatively random discoveries, such as a tight cluster of ten musket balls, five gunflints, and one die that probably had formerly been the contents of a

FIG. 4.7. Excavating the upper, eighteenth-century part of the midden at Site 2 in 1991. Facing south.

FIG. 4.8. Excavating under-neath the dredge in Trench 3 in 1991. Facing north.

FIG. 4.9. A very compact cluster of musket balls and gunflints found in Site 2, a short distance north of Dwelling 1.

leather or cloth pouch carried by a soldier or Ranger (fig. 4.9). And of course we found the prehistoric skeleton described in chapter 1.

Our most unusual discovery, though, came on the very first day of our dig, at Site 1. We decided to place one of our crews in the open field next to the flagpoles and monument that Earl Stott and his son had erected in 1964 (fig. 3.3). This appeared to be an undisturbed location, and we certainly wanted to avoid digging into any of the areas that had previously been dug by Earl and his friends. Within a few hours, the site supervisor, Dan Weiskotten, came to see me and announced, "They're finding tiny fragments of human bone all over the surface!" A few minutes later, Dan picked up a small bone and added, "That's a piece of human skull!"

Now that he had thoroughly gotten my attention, I walked over and noticed that, sure enough, there were hundreds of tiny, burned bone fragments scattered over the surface of the grass that had been mowed only a day or two before. Many pieces had already been collected, placed into plastic bags, and sent back to our field lab in the Fort Edward School for processing. These were clearly remains from a cremation, and as I thought for a minute, I remembered that Earl Stott had died the previous fall. I guessed, and it was later confirmed, that just a day before our dig started, Earl's family had carried his ashes out to his beloved island, looked for a place where they hoped we would never dig, and scattered his remains next to the two flagpoles. If we had known this, we most certainly would not have dug there!

Earl, who had so dearly loved discovering thousands of artifacts over the years, had now become hundreds of "artifacts" himself and was resting in plastic bags in our laboratory. There was only one thing to do, and I asked my diggers to "bring him back." We then returned Earl's ashes to the ground. Ironically, during the brief period that he resided in our lab, one of our volunteers had wanted to determine whether the white fragments she was looking at were bits of shellfish or bone. Using the age-old "taste test," she had put some of the bone fragments to her tongue and pronounced, "This isn't shell, this is bone!" At which point our lab supervisor, Barbara De Angelo, calmly informed her, "Yes, this is Earl." My poor volunteer, visibly agitated, couldn't do enough to try to wash out her mouth afterward! I have no doubt that Earl himself would have loved his transformation into artifacts to be found by the next generation.

1992 Research

We continued our work in 1992 in many of the same areas on Rogers Island and exposed much more of the storehouse (Site 1), which turned out to have been more than 90 feet long and 13 feet wide. A large, trash-filled latrine was discovered to the north, and it was later opened up in 1993. Prehistoric features underlay the military occupation everywhere at Site 1, including a huge firepit or "roasting platform" that was full of fire-cracked rocks, deer bones, and chert and quartzite flakes (fig. 1.11).

We dug more trenches through the dredge in the barracks area (Sites 11, 12, and 16). At Site 11 (Trench 2) we found a large brick fireplace inside the outline of a hut that I am referring to here as "Dwelling 2." This still had three east-west rows of nails from what had once been a well-built wood floor. The floor was now gone, but the nails remained vertical in the ground, embedded in the traces of wood that remained. In 1993, we further exposed this hut site, and it was unquestionably the most intact hut that we ever discovered on Rogers Island.

We continued our search, unsuccessfully, for the site of the smallpox hospital (Site 14), where we found both round and square posthole stains and several large features that contained burned wood, bricks, and hand wrought nails. We also found several prehistoric hearths in the hospital area, suggesting a very rich Native American site here at the southern end of the island.

In 1992 we dug many pits along the west side of the road that runs the length of Rogers Island. We found prehistoric hearths in Site 13 and more of the midden at Site 17 (our former Site 2), where rich military artifacts overlay a freshwater shell midden that contained prehistoric sherds, fire-cracked rocks, and much evidence of burning. The presence of prehistoric sites over most of Rogers Island was no doubt our most important finding during the 1992 season.

FIG. 4.10. Cathy Lee excavating a cluster of musket balls underneath the dirt floor of Dwelling 1.

1993 Research

A principal objective in 1993 was to bring some of our sites to closure, and we resumed digging at Dwelling 1 in Site 2, at Dwelling 2 in Site 11, at the latrine in Site 1, and in the smallpox hospital area. All these sites were rich in artifacts, and we also did a great deal of testing along the roadway and on the western side of the island (Site 6) in an effort to locate additional huts and dumps.

Dwelling 1 proved especially rewarding as we excavated deeper into the floor of the feature and found artifacts that had been dropped or discarded and trodden into the soft sand by soldiers living inside the tent. We found a brick scatter at the northeast corner of the tent, probably from a third fireplace, and discovered more vertical wood planks set against one side of a trench that ran around the perimeter of the feature. Just below the occupation floor there were scattered wine bottle fragments, a flattened canteen, a two-tined fork, a pewter spoon handle, and musket balls and gunflints. Most dramatically, there was a dense cache of forty-four musket balls lying just below the surface of the dirt floor in the northeast corner of the tent (fig. 4.10), as well as another scatter of eight musket balls that included a single gunflint. Also in the northeast corner, the site supervisor, Cathy Lee, found what she considered to have been a doorway, suggested by the pintle from a hinge and stains from traffic in and out of the building. We even found a tent peg ring and the metal base from a tent pole, evidence that this had been a tent rather than a hut, and suggesting that wood side walls had been added to make it more permanent and weatherproof.

At Dwelling 2 we finally located all the corners of the hut, and we also found a possible wood sill south of the fireplace that had been exposed in 1992. Because of the wood floor that had served as a seal under this building, there were very few artifacts that lay underneath, unlike the tent at Dwelling 1. And nearby, also in our Trench 2, we discovered two huge barracks fireplaces of brick, but we put off exposing these until 1994.

At Site 1 we finally were prepared to expose the latrine that was north of the storehouse, and part of this work was caught on film by New Dominion Pictures as they prepared a program for The Learning Channel. This large, dark stain with well-defined edges contained so many artifacts that clearly it had become a trash pit at the end of its use. Its contents included large metal artifacts, including two axes, many butchered animal bones, a fish hook, musket balls, buttons, and bottle glass. Curiously, there was much white residue that appeared to be lime inside the pit's outline, further supporting the idea that this had been a large privy.

Our search for the smallpox hospital on Rogers Island continued to be frustrating, and a 3-meter (north-south) by 20-meter (east-west) excavation trench failed to find any evidence for the building. However, a second excavation that we conducted just to the east was clearly inside a dump that lay on the edge of the raised terrace that once supported the hospital. This dump contained great quantities of butchered animal bones, a spade, a horseshoe, gunflints, cuff links, nails, and wine bottle glass. Best of all, we discovered a large fascine knife in the dump, bringing to mind historical sources that mention soldiers cutting fascines at the smallpox hospital. Underlying the eighteenth-century military part of the dump, we also found a shell midden that contained many prehistoric pottery sherds and part of a prehistoric pipe bowl. We did not yet have the outline of the hospital itself, but its terrace at the south end of the island was definitely proving to be a very rich occupation site.

Every one of the sites we investigated in 1993 had prehistoric artifacts mixed in, but we made our most unusual find at Site 11 (Trench 2), where we excavated a large pit that contained prehistoric pottery sherds close to the surface and a pair of deer antlers at the bottom (see chapter 1). With finds such as these, we increasingly realized that the story of Native peoples on Rogers Island needs to be told just as thoroughly as that of the soldiers who camped there in the 1750s.

1994 Research

Nineteen-ninety-four was the year that we found the smallpox hospital. It was wonderful! After three years of searching, we had all but given up, but Matt Rozell and a group of die-hard veteran diggers had doggedly returned each season to the terrace at the south end of Rogers Island. Even the first ten days in 1994 appeared bleak, but on July 15 two long, linear stains began to appear, and these met at a right angle at the northwest corner of the hospital complex. We interpreted these to be the remains of palisade walls that had flanked the hospital on the north and west. Later, we found two north-south rows of post molds, all that was left of the hospital's east and west walls (see chapter 6). This discovery was appreciated all the more because it had taken four confusing field seasons to finally find a structure that had been clearly marked on an engineer's map. But temporary structures supported by posts can leave very few traces behind. The extensive midden excavated in 1993 lay just to the east of the hospital outline and no doubt contained dumping from the hospital.

Even as Matt's team worked at the site of the smallpox hospital, a second crew focused on exposing the remains of one of the barracks buildings in Site 11. This building had been discovered underneath a great mound of river dredge (fig. 4.11). Traces of two large barracks fireplaces had begun appearing in 1993, and we completely exposed these in 1994. The more east-

FIG. 4.11. Ninety-year-old dredge from the Hudson River towers over the barracks area.

FIG. 4.12. Drawing a massive stone base or platform in the barracks area.

erly fireplace was exceptionally intact and had charcoal-filled fire channels that opened on both the east and west, whereas the more westerly fireplace was missing its upper courses of brick. We found great quantities of artifacts and burned bone fragments around each fireplace, but widespread probing did not reveal the use of stone foundations anywhere underneath the barracks. The log walls appear to have been built directly on the ground. Nevertheless, we did find a large stone base in the barracks area that had been mortared together, and this appeared to be the structural underpinning for a great fireplace or kiln (the surface was still covered with brick fragments) (fig. 4.12).

We also did a small amount of additional digging in Dwelling 1 (Site 2), where we went deeper in several of the test pits. We finally removed the hearths that we had exposed in previous years, but we left in situ all the board fragments that had formed low walls. Our deeper pits did reveal that the tent had been built atop a prehistoric shell midden.

1995 Research

In 1995 we moved our excavations to the site of the fort in Fort Edward because Rogers Island was on the market to be sold. However, a phone call from *Archaeology* magazine offered us the chance to appear for a second time in the series *Archaeology* on The Learning Channel if a crew could film us digging on the island. Fortunately, we received permission from the island's owners (who had not yet sold it) to proceed, and we decided to reopen the more intact barracks fireplace first exposed in 1994. This was definitely the most impressive and photogenic feature that The Learning Channel could possibly film. Over the space of several days we "redug" the fireplace, found a few additional artifacts around the edges, and showed a national television audience that Rogers Island has been the scene of some exciting archeology! (See the box "The Learning Channel Films on Rogers Island.")

1997 Research

Our return to Rogers Island in 1997 was at the request of a new property owner, and power equipment was then used to remove many tons of dredge from atop the barracks area. This enabled us to expose tents, huts, or barracks to which we had not previously had access. During the 1997 season, we identified the rich midden areas on the west edge of the island road as "Site 18," and pits near the barracks area (our old Site 11) were now called "Site 19."

One of our veteran diggers, Frank Bump, spearheaded the work at Site 18, and he went on to expose a shallow, dark midden with a mixture of both eighteenth-century and prehistoric artifacts. As work progressed, the site was found to contain a great many burned bones, nails, pipe stems, stoneware, delft and porcelain sherds, and a bone-inlaid knife handle. Much of the midden was burned to a bright red, and burning was concentrated in three patches, suggesting that soldiers had deliberately burned garbage there. While this feature was only about 10 centimeters thick and 1 meter across, the porcelain, bone-handled knife, and many pieces of glass tableware definitely suggest higher-status dumping, perhaps from an officers' hut.

Our work at Site 19 produced rather different results because we found stains, post molds, pits, and traces of huts or tents all around the perimeter of the barracks building exposed in 1994. In fact, there appeared to have been military occupations at three or more depths, confirming historical records indicating that soldiers repeatedly returned to Rogers Island to create new settlements. We also found great numbers of butchered animal bones here, scattered across a broad area, along with hundreds of nails, sherds, musket balls, gunflints, and a complete tobacco pipe. One of the larger stains at Site 19 began to form a clear outline in the sand, and this became our "Dwelling 3," another tent site.

★ The Learning Channel Films on Rogers Island

So many discoveries were made on Rogers Island in the 1990s that the series *Archaeology* on The Learning Channel went twice to Fort Edward to film our archeological work. This resulted in the 1993 program titled "The Last of the Mohicans" and the 1995 show titled "Rogers' Rangers," both based upon articles that I had published in *Archaeology* magazine. In each case it was New Dominion Pictures of Virginia Beach, Virginia, that prepared the script and did the filming, and Tom Naughton was the producer. Only thirty-nine shows were prepared over the span of three years, featuring archeological sites all over the world, so the two devoted to our work implies a status for Rogers Island that is roughly equivalent to Pompeii and the pyramids in Egypt! Seriously, though, this level of television coverage has helped to give Rogers Island a taste of the national recognition that it richly deserves.

Along with the film crews came reenactors, "expert" scholars, re-created military and Indian camps, and of course lots of "live," on-camera discoveries and interviews. Fort Edward never looked better! But there is no question that diverse television audiences do appreciate dynamic stories about early military history, and Rogers Island had some of the largest encampments of the eighteenth century.

Both programs on The Learning Channel were lively and enjoyable, and during the filming of "Rogers' Rangers," there definitely was a thrill in watching rugged men dressed in green creeping through the forest at night, on the verge of attacking and burning the re-created Abenaki village of St. Francis in Canada. As the reenactors burst into a clearing, Abenaki braves leaped from behind trees and uttered bloodcurdling yells as they defended their village. Over the course of many different takes, the Abenaki were killed dozens of times over, wigwams refused to burn, and smoke machines filled the forest with glorious gray swirls, looking rather like fog in a horror movie. Rogers Island had not seen this much action since the 1750s! Still, watching the reenactors at their craft suggested something more: the qualities that make them so effective—their zeal, spontaneity, and childlike passion for their hobby—are some of the very same qualities that we archeologists demonstrate while on our digs.

The team from New Dominion Pictures filming the remains of the latrine in Site 1.

FIG. 4.13. Rotted wood resting on the floor of Dwelling 5.

1998 Research

By 1998 we had exposed a more than adequate sample of the military sites on Rogers Island, and it was with some reluctance that we returned for one more season with a small group. We briefly examined the midden at Site 18 and finished it, and we spent the rest of the season at Site 19, exploring stains and features that had looked promising in 1997. Two of these were clearly the outlines of tents or huts, and one became our "Dwelling 4," whereas the other was simply too large to have been an ordinary hut. While we were still in the field, we began to refer to the large outline as the "Officers' House," but here I am referring to it as "Dwelling 5."

Dwelling 4 initially appeared to be a large trash pit because so many artifacts were lying on its surface, and these included so many butchered bones—especially from pigs—that we believe soldiers were throwing garbage onto the site after other soldiers had ceased to live there. As its outline took shape, this clearly was just a little bit smaller than our earlier Dwelling 1. It had scattered bricks and charcoal from a former hearth and a hard-packed dirt floor, so it clearly was a dwelling site and probably the remains of a tent.

Dwelling 5 (the "Officers' House") was a discovery we had made a few days before the close of the 1997 season. When we returned in 1998, we exposed much of a large, permanent structure with a wood floor and a substantial fireplace (fig. 4.13). There even was a dog burial on one side of it. This was clearly a hut, probably intended for year-round use, and considerably larger than the hut that I have termed "Dwelling 2."

With the close of the 1998 season, we knew that we had dug more than enough on Rogers Island, and there really were no other categories of sites left to explore. Yet increasingly, we were being urged by employees of the new owner of Rogers Island to dig *all* of each building, something that modern archeologists normally refuse to do unless a site is about to be destroyed. We decided to put a halt to any further excavation. A few months later, I asked the owner of the island, "Don't you want to leave something for the future?" The response was a resounding, "I don't want to leave nothing for the future! There are still artifacts there, aren't there?"

There are many reasons for doing archeology at sites from the French and Indian War, and Rogers Island no doubt has much more information to offer, but simply trying to obtain more artifacts is not a valid reason to dig. It clearly was time to complete our analysis and writing and to begin the process of interpretation.

Chapter 5

British and American
Military Architecture

HROUGHOUT OUR RESEARCH ON Rogers Island, we found
military dumps, badly disturbed fireplaces, and reddened earth in
practically every area where we dug. Such archeological features
are important to document and interpret, but we were even more eager
to locate and study the remains of military buildings, especially those
for which there is little historical record. Generally speaking, the best-
documented eighteenth-century military architecture is that of forts and
barracks, typically designed by engineers who were following standard
designs and who often left detailed drawings behind illustrating what they
planned to build. At the other extreme are the more vernacular structures
built by ordinary soldiers. These may have reflected building traditions
from their homes in the British Isles or from elsewhere in the colonies,
although some architectural elements may have been borrowed from Native Americans, and some may have been rough, makeshift designs created
by inexperienced builders who were just "making do" with available building materials.

When we commenced our excavations, I think I expected one type of
tent and one type of hut, relatively standardized in form, erected as temporary quarters for some soldiers, with other soldiers and officers living in
more permanent rooms in barracks buildings. In previous publications
about Rogers Island, I referred to all the smaller habitations we had excavated by the generic term "hut," but here I am using the more neutral term
"dwelling" to refer to all the types of simple huts and tents that were occupied by soldiers, officers, and rangers.

While it is tempting to identify each living site as a specific type, it is
probably better to think of soldiers' and officers' housing as a continuous
progression of types, ranging from a simple tent, to tents with chimneys
attached, to tents with boards added at ground level to keep in heat, to
tents/huts that had a wood floor (instead of hard-packed earth), to log
huts, all the way up to huts or houses that were sufficiently well built and

chinked that they might make it through several winters. Traditional historical sources do not deal with this range of building types, although Burt Loescher, John Cuneo, and Gary Zaboly have all published descriptions of what the appearance of ranger huts might have been. Cuneo, for example, wrote that "the Ranger huts were small, peak-roofed huts built adjacent to one another with common walls and holding either two or four men," and Loescher added that rangers "liked the mountain shack atmosphere of their huts and usually four Rangers of a congeniality would bunk in a hut." Neither Cuneo nor Loescher made direct use of archeological evidence, but Gary Zaboly has. Zaboly has presented very useful evidence for bark and brush having been common building materials during the French and Indian War, and his superb illustrations—in many different publications— have provided wonderful interpretations of the possible appearance(s) of cabins and huts.

General orders can also give useful insights into building types, as when General Lyman ordered on November 8, 1757, "That ye men belonging to ye Provensial troops take particular Cair not to pull Down or Distroy any of their Hutts upon Penalty of Staying here all winter." The soldiers' own diaries are perhaps the most helpful in describing the types of housing that were used. For example, Jabez Fitch, Jr., in 1757 made constant references to moving and pitching tents (and to visiting other officers in their tents!). But then, after commenting on how cold the weather had been, Fitch wrote on October 13, 1757, "This Day we went to work to Settle our tent in to ye Ground we Got our tent Pitchd this Day &c," and on October 14, "I Built a Chimny to our Tent." Clearly Fitch was "winterizing" his tent as the fall came on. Then, on December 11, he suddenly referred to how he "Kept at My Own Hutt." After that, all his references were to "my house" and "my hut," so clearly he had moved from a tent to a hut for the winter. While such references are extremely helpful, they unfortunately do not give exact descriptions or measurements for soldiers' and officers' housing, and much has to be inferred.

The archeologist has a difficult task in finding and interpreting military architecture in frontier settings because many structures were not built for permanency and it was easier to support a building's weight with posts, rather than to construct foundations. After all, a storehouse or hospital was often needed for only a season or two. In the specific case of Rogers Island, rows of tents and huts were constantly being pitched or constructed in close proximity to each other, thus creating large numbers of overlapping archeological sites. Building materials such as bricks would have been "raided" from earlier sites, and trash from later occupations was thrown on top of the remains of tents or huts from just a year before. Consequently, few sites can be studied in isolation, and artifacts that appear to be associated with a particular structure and its occupants may simply be trash thrown there later by someone else.

d, 1991–1998

es, solitary post molds,
ambiguous soil stains
nd. Unfortunately, the
classify a feature into a
preserved buildings and
hospital is discussed in

e base of the monument
ig. 5.1), we did not expect

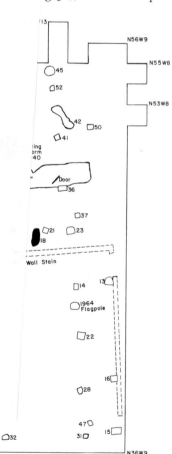

FIG. 5.1. A plan view of the storehouse at Site 1, displaying just the prehistoric and historic features that were excavated. Features are identified as follows:

Historic post molds: 3B, 4, 9–10, 13–16, 19–24, 28–32, 36–37, 41, 43, 46–47, 49–52
Historic trash pit: 6, 11, 33
Prehistoric firepits: 1, 2, 3A, 7, 25–27, 44, 48
Prehistoric trash pit: 5, 8, 12, 18
Prehistoric "Roasting Platform": 38–40
Tree stain: 34, 45
Rodent activity: 35
Unknown: 17, 42

FIG. 5.2. A fragment from a wood door found inside the storehouse (Site 1).

to find remains of a rectangular, post-type building underneath. Yet in 1991 and 1992, teams led by Dan Weiskotten excavated a large structure in the center of Rogers Island that had utilized posts at about 8-foot intervals along its perimeter. This building had originally been 13 feet wide (between posts), and after extending some pits to the north, Dan determined that it had been more than 90 feet long. Part of a wood door was found inside a large feature or "pit" underneath this site (fig. 5.2), and we often found that the large, square, dark post molds were full of historic period trash. This included many rosehead nails and butchered bone fragments; wine bottle and medicine vial fragments; tobacco pipe fragments; and sherds of porcelain, delft, white salt-glazed stoneware, unrefined stoneware, and buff-bodied, slip-decorated earthenware. There were in fact more sherds of porcelain inside the storehouse than anywhere else on the island. There also were small numbers of gunflints, musket balls, buckshot, and metal buttons (see table 7.2).

We did not find any evidence for a fireplace inside the building, although we did find prehistoric trash pits and firepits almost everywhere underneath the former structure. The temporary nature of this style of construction, coupled with the absence of fireplaces and the dimensions of the long, narrow building, all tend to favor its identification as a storehouse. I do not know whether this was the "large storehouse" that contemporary historical accounts placed on Rogers Island, but I believe that it probably was.

Some of the large, square post molds still contained the rotting bases of posts. Other post molds contained trash, placed there after the posts had been removed, or else used as chinking when posts were first placed in their

FIG. 5.3. The cross section of a post mold at the storehouse. A large, butchered bone is exposed in the profile.

holes (fig. 5.3). We made several distinctive finds within the storehouse, including an intact tin bucket, amputated finger bones from a human hand, a thimble, a bayonet fragment, a fish hook, and British halfpennies dating to 1734 and 1757. The presence of 146 fragments of window glass suggests that windows were in use, although window glass may have been stored here for use elsewhere in the camp.

The Latrine (Site 1)

Dan Weiskotten's team extended shovel test pits out in all directions from the storehouse site, looking for associated features, and in late 1992 an exploratory trench to the north located a dark, trash-filled feature that was absolutely packed with artifacts. We returned to the site in 1993, and as we excavated down, a rectangular outline took shape that measured about 8 feet east-west by 4 feet north-south (figs. 5.4 and 5.5). We initially referred to this as a trash pit, but later decided that with its sharply cut, vertical walls it was more likely to have been a latrine or "necessary." We excavated this feature in four large quadrants and took it down to sterile soil with trowels.

The more distinctive artifacts in this feature included some 8,804 butchered animal bones, 45 musket balls, 39 metal buttons, 7 bone buttons, 73 fragments of glass vials, many fragments of tobacco pipes, wine bottles, and pottery sherds, and two large felling axes. The variety of artifact types was most impressive, and whether or not this pit began as a latrine, it definitely saw final use as a trash pit (see table 7.2).

FIG. 5.4. The surface outline of the latrine (Site 1).

FIG. 5.5. Sarah van Ryckevorsel excavating one of the quadrants of the latrine.

Huts and Tents

DWELLING 1 (SITE 2)

One of the best-preserved examples of a living site is a tent that we unearthed over the course of 1991, 1993, and 1994. We exposed the remains of several vertical wood planks that had once formed walls around the dwelling (fig. 5.6), and over the course of three seasons we found scattered bricks and ashes from three fireplaces. Inside the outline formed by the vertical planks, there were traces of an earth floor, compressed by soldiers' feet into a very hard surface (fig. 5.7). This structure was perhaps the same sort of "winterized" tent that Jabez Fitch, Jr., described in his journal.

If about four soldiers or rangers once lived here, then they were huddled into an area that measured only about 11.2 by 12.4 feet. Scattered atop this living floor we discovered burned bits of bone, burned clay, rosehead nails, lead slag, a silver shoe buckle, a pewter spoon, and even a Spanish silver cob.

When we returned to Dwelling 1 in 1993, we extended the excavation to the east and also went deeper into the sand. There were rich caches of mus-

FIG. 5.6. Cross-sectioning some of the vertical wood planking in Dwelling 1.

FIG. 5.7. The surface outline of Dwelling 1, showing its appearance at the end of the excavation in 1991. The staining and vertical wall planks around the perimeter have been outlined with yarn. Facing north.

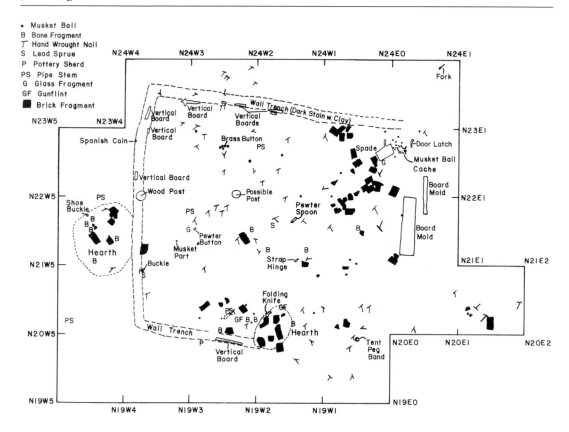

- Musket Ball
B Bone Fragment
T Hand Wrought Nail
S Lead Sprue
P Pottery Sherd
PS Pipe Stem
G Glass Fragment
GF Gunflint
■ Brick Fragment

FIG. 5.8. A plan view of Dwelling 1 at the completion of the three years of excavation.

ket balls and gunflints that had been pressed into the floor, and there also were knives, forks, spoons, wine bottles and some 662 fragments of butchered, burned bone. There was one cluster of 44 musket balls, but more common were clusters of 9 or 10 musket balls, along with a few gunflints. Altogether there were 74 musket balls of various types but not much pottery (see table 7.1).

A small amount of additional digging was conducted here in 1994, and figure 5.8 shows nearly everything that we discovered over the three years we worked here. While the western edge of the tent site was fairly intact, the eastern side was more disturbed and harder to interpret.

DWELLING 2 (SITE 11)

In 1993 we discovered an unusually intact and relatively permanent structure at the western end of Site 11. Dwelling 2 measured 11.4 by 13 feet, and it still contained evidence for three rows of nails where floor boards had been nailed down onto the joists underneath (figs. 5.9 and 5.10). At its northern end, Dwelling 2 had a well-built brick fireplace that was still in excellent condition (fig. 5.11), but there were very few artifacts inside the footprint of this building. Unlike Dwelling 1, this site had had a wood floor,

FIG. 5.9. The excavation of Dwelling 2, with its fireplace at the rear. Facing northwest.

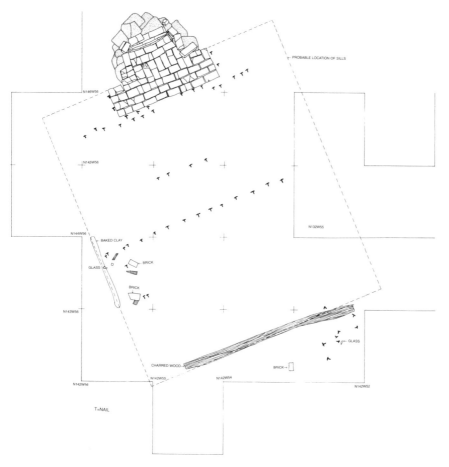

FIG. 5.10. A plan view of Dwelling 2. Courtesy of Dennis E. Howe.

PROBABLE LOCATION OF SILLS

N146W56

N145W56

N144W56

BAKED CLAY

GLASS

BRICK

BRICK

N143W56

N132W55

N142W56

CHARRED WOOD

N142W55

N142W54

BRICK

GLASS

N142W52

T=NAIL

FIG. 5.11. The brick fireplace in Dwelling 2. Facing west.

which had prevented artifacts from being pressed into the underlying sand. If the building had been swept out periodically, there would be no reason for artifacts to be left behind, and in fact Dwelling 2 contained the fewest artifacts of any structure we examined (see table 7.1).

DWELLING 3 (SITE 19)

In 1997 we found the outline of another tent (fig. 5.12), this one on the southern edge of the barracks building we had exposed in 1994. Unlike Dwelling 1, there was no evidence of wood planks forming lower walls, but the extent of the staining revealed that this tent had measured about 7.6 by 8.4 feet. There was no clear evidence for a fireplace in the interior. The northwest corner had a well-defined post mold, where a spade had cut very sharp edges into the ground. Once the perimeter of this feature had been exposed, we then divided the entire structure into four quadrants for final excavation and plotted in the artifacts (fig. 5.13).

Dwelling 3 contained quite a few sherds of redware and delft, as well as tobacco pipes, but the total artifact counts were quite low. Food remains were well represented by some 1,321 fragments of butchered bone, and armaments—while not abundant—included gunflints, musket balls, lead slag, and buckshot (see table 7.1). This was perhaps a short-term habitation site representing but a single season.

DWELLING 4 (SITE 19)

We found the complete outline of yet another tent in 1998, northeast of the barracks complex. There was a very impressive scatter of brick fragments

FIG. 5.12. The surface outline of Dwelling 3 in 1997. Its perimeter has been outlined with string, and the corner post mold is visible at the upper right. Facing west.

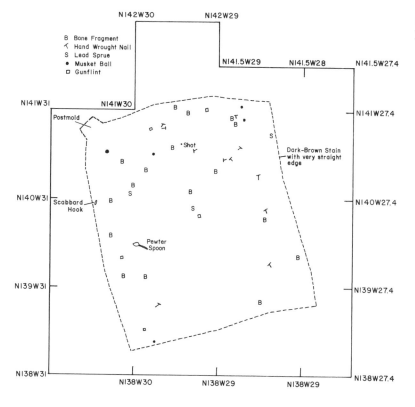

FIG. 5.13. A plan view of Dwelling 3.

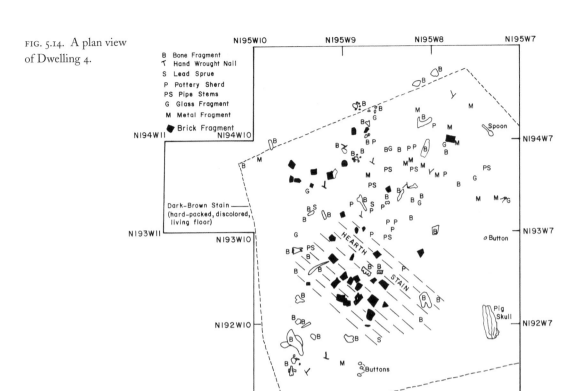

FIG. 5.14. A plan view of Dwelling 4.

B   Bone Fragment
┳   Hand Wrought Nail
S   Lead Sprue
P   Pottery Sherd
PS Pipe Stems
G   Glass Fragment
M   Metal Fragment
◆   Brick Fragment

Dark-Brown Stain
(hard-packed, discolored,
living floor)

HEARTH
STAIN

Spoon
Button
Pig
Skull
Buttons

FIG. 5.15. Fred Harris excavating the living floor of Dwelling 4. The surface is thoroughly littered with bricks and butchered animal bones. Facing west.

FIG. 5.16. The pig skull
discovered at the southeast
corner of Dwelling 4.

former fireplace, and there was much associated char-
of this dwelling was clear and dark, it
side, and the surface was covered
of everything else (fig. 5.15). We
in the southeast corner (fig. 5.16),
sherds (chiefly delft), many wine
1746 British halfpenny, and plenty
balls (see table 7.1). The occupants
lture, and while there were no signs
much more substantive occupation

n, two of our veteran diggers, Bill Her-
a rich scatter of artifacts at the eastern
esolved to return and explore the spot in
ered with pieces of wood and gunflints,
musket balls,   sherds of delft and white salt-glazed
stoneware. As excavations proceeded in 1998, linear stains began to outline
where the outer walls had been, and we exposed a very sizable fireplace at
the southeast corner of the building (fig. 5.18). The remains of a wood floor
were everywhere—although it was extremely rotted—and there also were
vertical boards jutting up at several points on the perimeter (fig. 5.19). This
very well built structure measured about 16.6 by 17.4 feet, and the quality
and quantity of its artifacts led us to keep referring to it as the "Officers'
House," even though it may simply have been a year-round dwelling.

FIG. 5.17. The excavation of Dwelling 5 in 1998. The brick fireplace is in the foreground. Facing north.

FIG. 5.18. The fireplace inside Dwelling 5. Facing west.

The artifacts included two pieces of gold braid, an axe (fig. 5.20), a spade (fig. 5.21), many sherds of delft and other ceramics, wine bottles, a 1723 British halfpenny, many tobacco pipe fragments, and 1,488 butchered bone fragments (see table 7.1). This hut was exceptional in its integrity and in the richness of its artifacts, and we dug perhaps two-thirds of the site before deciding that the rest of it should be preserved for the future.

DWELLING 6 (SITE 3)

A team headed by Dennis Howe was working north of the barracks area in 1991 when they discovered a living floor that he believed represented the remains of a tent site (fig. 5.22). There was a large looter's intrusion near the center of the area, but the dark stains here suggested a floor much like that in Dwelling 1. We did not find any staining or boards forming a clear out-

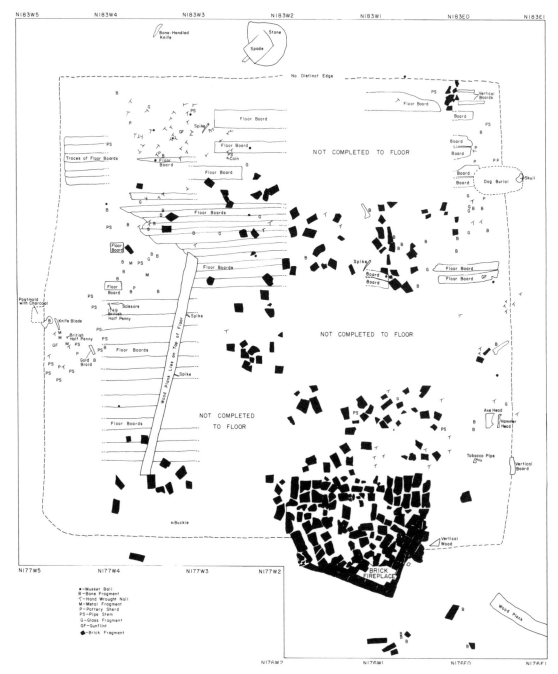

FIG. 5.19. A plan view of Dwelling 5.

FIG. 5.20. A large axe discovered just inside the eastern wall of Dwelling 5.

FIG. 5.21. The complete blade from a spade, discovered just north (and outside) of Dwelling 5. Facing north.

line for this tent, so no dimensions could be obtained. The tip from a tent pole (referred to in the plan as a "wrought iron pike tip") was found driven vertically into the ground, suggesting that it had once held up a tent or awning here. Brick fragments to the north suggested a disturbed fireplace, so a temporary dwelling is the most likely interpretation. Still, like the tent at Dwelling 3, this is a very ephemeral site.

Armaments were quite common here, including 21 musket balls, and there were 624 fragments of butchered bone, a bone-handled knife (fig. 5.23), as well as 10 metal buttons, much pottery, and many pieces of wine bottles (see table 7.1).

The Barracks on Rogers Island

Over the years that the Rogers Island Historical Association worked on Rogers Island, the members and helpers researched engineers' maps and had a good sense of where the barracks buildings had been. Their search was especially aided by the fact that the barracks were always portrayed directly to the west of the fort. From the very beginning, they often used power equipment to move the massive dredge piles out of the way.

When our work began in 1991, we benefited from consulting historical maps, from the work of the association, and from surface evidence. We knew that the barracks had the potential to be the richest sites of all because of the length of occupation and the massiveness of the architecture. Contemporary military maps portrayed the barracks buildings as two-story structures with outside staircases and central fireplaces. The barracks were

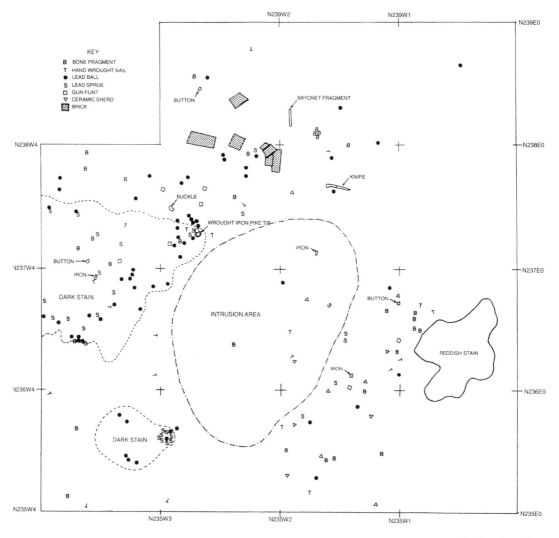

KEY
B BONE FRAGMENT
T HAND WROUGHT NAIL
● LEAD BALL
S LEAD SPRUE
□ GUN FLINT
▽ CERAMIC SHERD
▨ BRICK

BUTTON

BAYONET FRAGMENT

KNIFE

BUCKLE

WROUGHT IRON PIKE TIP

IRON

BUTTON

IRON

DARK STAIN

INTRUSION AREA

BUTTON

REDDISH STAIN

IRON

DARK STAIN

FIG. 5.22. A plan view of Dwelling 6. Courtesy of Dennis E. Howe.

FIG. 5.23. The bone-handled knife and associated musket balls discovered on the floor of Dwelling 6. Facing south.

constructed in two long north-south lines, with each building abutting other barracks buildings to either the north or the south (see fig. 2.1). Contemporary British engineers' drawings showed that only two barracks ran east-west *across* the island, at the northern and southern extremes of the barracks complex.

In 1993 we discovered a large barracks fireplace base of brick (figs. 5.24 and 5.25), and excavations in 1994 revealed a second massive brick fireplace base (figs. 5.26 and 5.27), about 45 feet from the first (fig. 5.28). Both fire-

FIG. 5.24. Don Thompson excavating the more westerly barracks fireplace in 1994. The upper courses of bricks had been completely removed, probably by past plowing. Facing south.

FIG. 5.25. A plan view of the more westerly barracks fireplace.

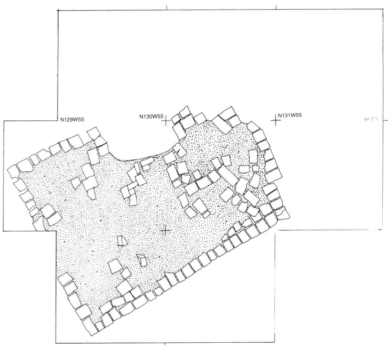

FIG. 5.26. Excavating the more easterly barracks fireplace in 1994. Facing west.

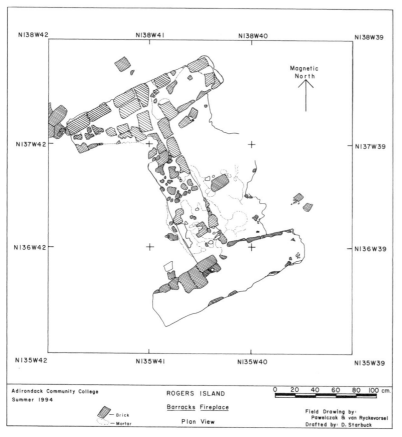

FIG. 5.27. A plan view of the more easterly barracks fireplace.

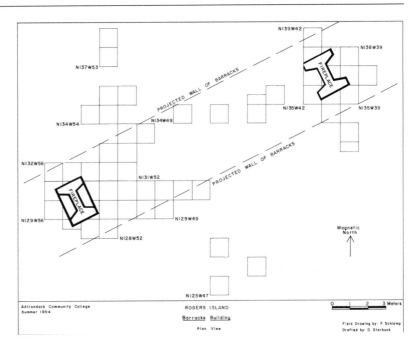

FIG. 5.28. A schematized outline of the barracks building excavated in 1993–1994.

places had been within a single east-west building, and both were two-sided, opening on both the east and the west. While we initially believed that this was the most southern barracks building, it now appears from historical maps to be much more likely that this was the foundation for the northernmost barracks.

Of the two barracks fireplaces, the second one proved to be much more intact and also was surrounded by many more artifacts. These included great numbers of tobacco pipes—far more than inside the huts or tents we excavated—as well as many armaments, pottery sherds, and 3,332 butchered bone fragments (see table 7.2). We failed to find an outer edge to the barracks building, even after opening up many adjacent pits, but the rotted logs really should have left some staining in the soil.

Final Thoughts

It is difficult to reduce the many hundreds of buildings that once stood on Rogers Island to just a handful of site descriptions. Still, these are the most intact sites that have survived archeologically from the many rows of tents and huts and from the several large barracks buildings that stood on Rogers Island in the 1750s. There are no doubt additional fireplaces, tent stains, and hut outlines on the island that can still be found archeologically, but much of what was once there has been destroyed during past digs. We found far too many piles of discarded bricks, suggesting that extensive areas on Rogers Island have been overdug.

The hut and tent sites that we discovered may well have been constructed in rows initially, but so much has been removed over the years that we could no longer tell whether our sites were isolated or in rows. We also could not date any of them precisely, so it is impossible to say whether our Dwellings 1 through 6 were constructed before, during, or after the massive barracks buildings went up on the island. However, it would appear archeologically that these small structures were built just about everywhere, in between the more massive barracks structures.

Chapter 6

Evidence for Early Health Care on Rogers Island: The Search for the Smallpox Hospital

Introduction

SMALLPOX HAS OFTEN been described as the most dreaded disease in human history. Once pustules developed on the surface of the skin, death typically followed between ten and fourteen days later. The smallpox virus left most of its traces, the characteristic pockmarking, on the victim's face, where it destroyed the sebaceous glands. Afterward, the wounds in the skin often became infected, resulting in additional deaths. While quite a variety of opium-based medicines were available for treating other ailments in the eighteenth century, there was no cure for smallpox until the 1790s.

However, the eighteenth century saw important steps toward the curtailment of this disease, and smallpox inoculation was introduced into Europe and North America in 1721. Self-inoculation was common among soldiers on the frontier, although this practice was frequently banned because of the risk of spreading the virus. One of the most severe outbreaks of the disease was in 1775–1776 as the Continental Army lay siege to Quebec City. In the following year General George Washington wrote to William Shippen, the newly appointed director-general of the Continental Army Medical Department, insisting that the army be inoculated.

Not long afterward, an English physician, Edward Jenner, noticed that milkmaids had very clear complexions and did not get smallpox. In his subsequent experiments he vaccinated using the cowpox virus, and thus established that milkmaids' contact with cows' udders had, in effect, inoculated them (through cracks in their hands). Jenner published his *Inquiry into the Causes and Effects of Variola Vaccinae* in London in 1798, but it took much longer to eradicate smallpox altogether.

The world's last reported case of endemic smallpox, *Variola minor*, was discovered in Somalia in 1977, and the Global Commission for the Certifi-cation of Smallpox Eradication finally certified the eradication of the dis-ease in 1979. (Laboratory samples of the virus still exist in Atlanta, Georgia, and in Russia.) It required much systematic effort and willpower to con-quer the smallpox virus, and doctors today tend to compare it with the HIV virus that causes AIDS, suggesting that it will take just as much effort to eradicate this new killer. Still, the smallpox virus is remarkably resistant to extermination, even outside the body.

The Search for the Smallpox Hospital on Rogers Island

The military hospitals on Rogers Island were of several types, including the "Great Blockhouse" that was converted into a hospital, assorted barracks' rooms that were used for patients, and a smallpox hospital that was posi-tioned at the southern end of the island, as far from the main barracks com-plex as possible. Of the several hospitals, the smallpox hospital appeared the most promising for archeological research because it had stood alone on top of a raised terrace that reduced the hazard of flooding by the Hudson River. Its isolation also meant there was little danger of confusing its remains with those from any surrounding buildings.

Several of the diaries kept by soldiers living on Rogers Island make refer-ence to the island's smallpox hospital. For example, we know from the diary of Jabez Fitch, Jr., that he and twenty of his fellow soldiers constructed the smallpox hospital, beginning on May 31, 1757, "on ye Loar End of ye Island." A few days later they completed it, as noted by Fitch on June 2:

> In ye Morning Early I Went into ye Fort For Some Nails To Finish ye Hos-pital Then I Went over to ye Island with 10 Men Got Some Tools Came to ye Plais There was a Dutch Boy & a Young Woman a Milking Som Cows &c — Then we Finished ye Hospital and Returned Home

An addition was made to the hospital in 1758, and its exact location was later drawn on Thomas Mante's "Plan of Fort Edward and its environs on Hudsons River," engraved in 1772 and now in the Catalog of Kings Maps in the British Museum (fig. 1.1).

Because the hospital was in use for a couple of years and had sizable numbers of patients (another soldier, Luke Gridley, mentioned 101 men with smallpox on July 4, 1757), we were hopeful that considerable archeo-logical evidence would have survived. Still, we did not expect to find med-icines for treating smallpox. None are known to have existed at that time, and it was not until the American Revolution that inoculations against smallpox began on a more regular basis. We also do not know where the dead from the hospital were buried, although it does not appear that it was

FIG. 6.1. Overview of the excavation in the smallpox hospital area (Site 14) in 1992. Facing west.

anywhere on Rogers Island, perhaps because frequent spring flooding by the Hudson River might have washed out soldiers' bodies.

No traces of the smallpox hospital had survived on the surface of Rogers Island, but we did see evidence indicating where Earl Stott had used power equipment to search for it in the 1960s. The hospital proved to be incredibly elusive, however, and we ultimately needed four field seasons before we were positive we had found its outline. As our work progressed, light sampling in 1991 was inconclusive, so we used power equipment to scrape the surface of the terrace in 1992 (fig. 6.1). This more intensive approach revealed stains in the subsoil, at which time we found evidence for prehistoric hearths (figs. 6.2 and 6.3) and pottery on the terrace, as well as a Late Woodland shell midden (fig. 6.4). In 1993 another crew gave up in frustration after digging a 3-by-20-meter trench and believing (wrongly) that nothing was there. Our first good evidence, though, was a sizable dump that we discovered on the eastern edge of the raised terrace in 1993, containing an iron fascine knife with tang (22½ inches long and marked "LE" on the blade) (fig. 6.5), a modified iron barrel hoop, an iron horseshoe (fig. 6.6), hundreds of butchered animal bones, wine bottle fragments, but-

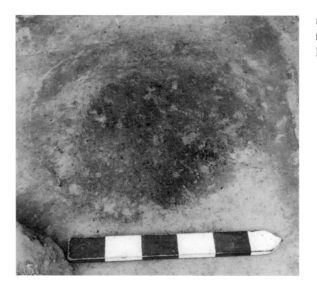

FIG. 6.2. Charcoal staining on the surface of a prehistoric hearth in Site 14. Facing west.

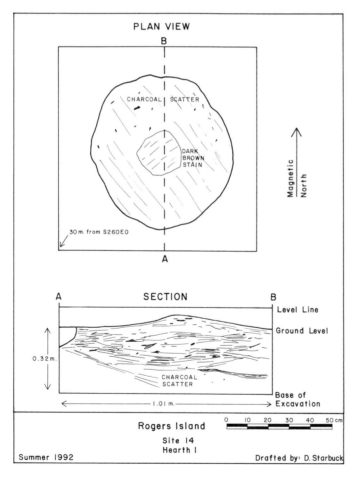

FIG. 6.3. A plan view and section through the prehistoric hearth in fig. 6.2.

PLAN VIEW

B

CHARCOAL SCATTER

DARK
BROWN
STAIN

Magnetic
North

30 m. from S260E0

A

SECTION

A   B

Level Line

Ground Level

0.32 m.

CHARCOAL
SCATTER

Base of
Excavation

1.01 m.

0   10   20   30   40   50 cm

Rogers Island
Site 14
Hearth 1

Summer 1992   Drafted by: D. Starbuck

FIG. 6.4. A prehistoric pottery sherd found in s283w1 inside the shell midden at Site 14.

FIG. 6.5. A fascine knife, used for clearing brush, discovered in the dump at Site 14.

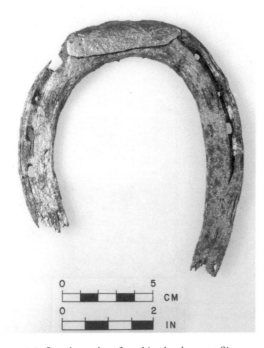

FIG. 6.6. Iron horseshoe found in the dump at Site 14.

FIG. 6.7. The northwest corner of the palisade line that borders the smallpox hospital on the north and west. Facing east.

tons, knives, a pair of copper cuff links with linen thread still attached, a bowl from a pewter spoon, a 1751 Spanish one-real piece, a 1753 British halfpenny, gunflints, and more. The only artifacts that suggested a hospital function were a few glass medicine vial fragments, but at least we had established that there had been a large occupation close by.

The 1994 season proved much more rewarding when dark, linear stains began to appear atop the terrace, outlining a trench or palisade line that ran for over 130 feet north-south along the western side of the terrace; it then made a right-hand turn (figs. 6.7 and 6.8) and ran another 58 feet east-west across the northern end of the terrace. While the outlines of individual posts were not discovered within this staining, it appeared that this had been a ditch into which palisade posts were set. (In *Old Fort Edward*, William Hill described palisades in the Fort Edward area as constructed of ten- to twelve-foot-long logs sharpened to a point before being set into a trench that was about three feet deep.) The staining we found was full of rosehead nails and charcoal flecks, and inside the western stain we discovered the complete 12-by-6-inch-wide blade from a spade (fig. 6.9), perhaps the very tool that had dug the palisade trench! In the center of the northern stain there was a "gap" of just over 3 feet, suggesting a possible doorway or entrance, and an iron key was in fact discovered just outside the opening. The northern and western palisade trenches contained relatively few artifacts, but there were two bandage pins, some butchered animal bones, and two sherds of white salt-glazed stoneware that appeared to come from a medicine cup. We still do not know why these two palisade walls were erected here, unless to ensure that the rest of the encampment did not have to view the sick and dying soldiers.

Using the trench stains and the eastern dump as possible outer limits for the hospital building, we did extensive testing within these limits, which ultimately revealed two north-south rows of post molds forming the eastern and western sides of a building whose weight had rested upon posts (figs. 6.10 and 6.11). We had not expected to find substantial foundations, and indeed there was no evidence that any stone had been used as footings for the structure. This type of temporary construction seems appropriate to a building thrown up hastily by soldiers. The 12-inch-square post molds were positioned at 5-foot intervals, outlining a structure that had been 15 feet wide. Each post mold contained traces of wood and charcoal, and we uncovered the dark stains from six hewn posts on either side of the building. It thus appears we exposed just the midsection of the hospital, an area that measured 15 feet east-west by 30 feet north-south. At the southernmost end of the building we found the remains of a hearth with fragments of brick and burnt sherds of delft inside it. Matthew Rozell, who supervised the 1994 excavation at the smallpox hospital, believes that the hospital was originally at least 80 feet long but that river flooding,

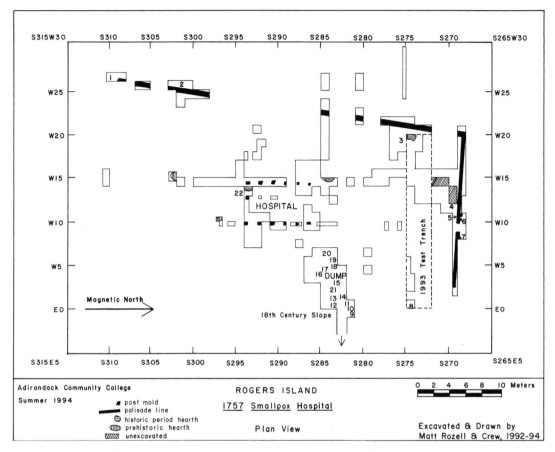

FIG. 6.8. Plan view of the smallpox hospital on Rogers Island. Artifacts and features are located as follows:

1. Spade blade, 12.5 × 6.25 inches, found within palisade stain
2. Two metal bandage pins, one straight and one hooked
3. Historic period hearth with two whole bricks, one large brick fragment, and burned bone
4. Square iron band
5. Broken brass ring with blue glass inlay, found within palisade stain
6. One complete iron key, found near gateway
7. One chisel-tipped rosehead spike, 4⅝16 inches long
8. One clear glass vial fragment
9. One clear glass vial fragment
10. One complete horseshoe
11. One round pewter spoon bowl
12. Modified iron barrel hoop, hooked on each end, probably converted into a pothook
13. English 1753 halfpenny (George II)
14. Modified, burned pewter spoon, with bowl folded inward
15. Dense concentration of butchered animal bones
16. Iron fascine knife with tang, 22.5 inches long; marked "LE"
17. One brass buckle, 1 × 1.25 inches
18. Spanish 1751 silver real
19. Square iron band
20. One triangular brass tinkler
21. One pair of copper cuff links, with linen thread intact
22. Historic period hearth (containing a burned delft sherd)

FIG. 6.9. The blade of a spade found in
s311w27, inside the palisade trench around
the smallpox hospital. Facing east.

FIG. 6.10. The two sides of the smallpox hospital, defined by post
molds.

FIG. 6.11. Post molds along one
side of the smallpox hospital.
These dark stains appeared at
the top of the subsoil and measured about 12 inches square.
Positioned at 5-foot intervals
and containing bits of wood
and charcoal, they clearly mark
the perimeter of a building that
was about 15 feet wide.

cultivation, and treasure hunting may have destroyed evidence for some of its outline.

In the fine yellow sand of Rogers Island there was no evidence of room divisions within the smallpox hospital, nor did we discover any evidence of how smallpox was being treated. However, we did find that the very rich body of artifacts in the associated dump was different in one very significant category from the artifacts found in dwellings on Rogers Island. Ceramics were almost totally missing from this assemblage. When intrusive sherds of whiteware are excluded from the count, only 12 pottery sherds were discovered in the entire hospital assemblage. This is significant because the dump contained some 2,818 butchered bone fragments—suggesting that plenty of food (meat) was being consumed here—and there were ample fragments of wine bottles and fragments from two pewter spoons, at least hinting at the process of food consumption. But there simply were no dishes to eat from. This may suggest that the sick and dying were eating from wood trenchers, but it could also mean that their dishes (and probably their clothing too) were being discarded in pits after use because of the fear of contamination.

The presence of a single medicine bottle fragment in the dump clearly does not prove the proximity of a hospital, because we know that soldiers typically took medicines back to their cabins. However, we do feel confident that this long, narrow building, which had been raised on posts, was the smallpox hospital; the evidence from diaries, maps, and now archeology is overwhelming. When we finished our work, we also left enough of the site intact that future archeologists may someday continue exposing the outline of the hospital and its associated dump.

Potential Hazards from Smallpox

While we were excavating the smallpox hospital on Rogers Island, local doctors would occasionally visit us and ask whether our students were in any danger of contracting the disease. I would invariably say no but I cannot say that I was totally sure of this. It was not until later that it became clear that smallpox would have needed tissue in which to survive, and decomposition would have been very rapid in the sandy soil on Rogers Island. So we really were in no danger.

After the attack upon the World Trade Center on September 11, 2001, there was renewed interest in whether smallpox could be used as a weapon by terrorists, and Chris Carola at the Associated Press office in Albany interviewed me for a news release dealing with this question. Because no one else had ever excavated a smallpox hospital, our work, ironically, had become extremely relevant to modern world issues. And while there is no danger that strains of smallpox from Rogers Island could ever be reintroduced to the world, the same cannot be said for the more recent cases of smallpox in Africa. It would be very easy to dig up any of the 1970s victims from a cemetery in Africa and to use their remains as a highly lethal source of the disease.

Other Evidence for Health Care on Rogers Island

The hospital function of Rogers Island, and of the whole military encampment in Fort Edward, was extremely important, and sick and injured soldiers were sent there from many other sites. While it is unknown exactly where the other hospitals were on the island, the frequency of several artifact types has sometimes been used as evidence for the presence of sick or wounded soldiers. These include glass medicine bottles (fig. 6.12), ceramic medicine cups, chewed musket balls (perhaps clenched between the teeth of hospital patients), and tobacco pipes marked with red paint (sometimes said to have been used by smallpox patients). All these artifacts have been found scattered throughout many contexts on Rogers Island, and none automatically suggests the presence of a hospital.

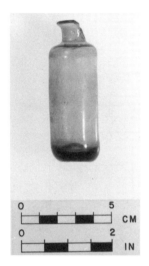

FIG. 6.12. A glass medicine bottle discovered in Site 19 (Dwelling 5) in 1998.

Although it is impossible to substantiate some of Earl Stott's claims, because of the lack of record keeping, he nevertheless stated during an interview with *Adirondack Life* magazine in 1986 that he had found a hospital on Rogers Island, and that it contained "countless brass 'hospital pins' . . . medicine bottles, a surgeon's scalpel in a brass case, an amputating saw, measuring spoons, a pill tile, two blown-glass inkwells, and not far from the building perimeter, a grisly cache of human toe bones—relics of frostbite victims." This "hospital" was supposed to have been the site of the "Great Blockhouse," built in 1756, that Earl believed he had excavated in 1966. Earl went on in the same interview to make an even more dramatic claim. The article states that he found a refuse pit with "traces of wool fabric, quicklime, 117 uniform buttons, 22 silver coins, clasp knives, and buckles. Stott says these are the remnants of fouled, bloodied clothing that had been cut from the bodies of sick or wounded men. 'No one dared go through the pockets to remove coins or other items.'" Earl believed that this clothing had been worn by the wounded from Abercrombie's ill-fated 1758 expedition to Fort Ticonderoga. While it is not now possible to verify any of these identifications and interpretations, all I can say is that we did not find anything comparable during our own (1991–1998) excavations on Rogers Island.

Chapter 7

Historical Artifacts Discovered on Rogers Island in the 1990s

Artifacts Unearthed on Rogers Island before 1991

*N*O QUANTITATIVE INFORMATION exists for any of the artifacts that were excavated by Earl Stott or the Rogers Island Historical Association between 1960 and 1988. The only general description of that collection appears in *Exploring Rogers Island*, but that volume was written in the late 1960s, prior to a great many of Earl's discoveries. During interviews, Earl tended to describe armaments, with little description of ceramics, glass, or food remains, and it may never be possible to prepare a complete artifact catalog of his finds. This is unfortunate, and it demonstrates all too well that archeological sites must never be dug unless there is adequate provision for analysis, cataloging, and writing afterward.

Artifacts Found During the 1990s

Throughout our excavations on Rogers Island, we maintained a summer field laboratory in Fort Edward, and for most years this was located inside the Mobil Oil Company building that later was converted into the Rogers Island Visitors Center. Experienced volunteers and students processed artifacts there in the summer months, and the process of artifact identification typically lasted throughout the winter so that we would be caught up with analysis before the start of the next field season. Artifacts were listed on forms that later became the basis for lengthy computer catalogs. At the final stage, Sarah Majot and Karl Hemker, Jr., of ARCH TECH converted the older catalogs into Excel documents so that the data could be manipulated more easily.

The results of these identifications are summarized in tables 7.1 and 7.2, and further summaries are presented as bar graphs in Appendixes 1 (artifact

Table 7.1

Artifacts Recovered from Dwellings on Rogers Island, 1991–1998

	Dwelling 1 (tent)	Dwelling 2 (hut)	Dwelling 3 (tent)	Dwelling 4 (tent)	Dwelling 5 (hut)	Dwelling 6 (tent)
Ceramic sherds						
Redware	7	4	122	6	9	8
Delft	4	2	32	78	109	12
Delft, burned	0	0	0	0	1	0
Buff-bodied slipware	0	0	0	0	1	2
Earthenware, burned	0	0	1	2	4	1
White salt-glazed stoneware	2	19	10	34	35	1
w. scratch blue	1	0	1	0	26	0
Gray salt-glazed stoneware	3	1	14	3	2	0
w. scratch blue	2	0	1	0	2	0
Brown stoneware	1	0	0	0	0	0
Unrefined stoneware	22	0	1	0	4	8
Unrefined stoneware, burned	0	0	0	0	8	0
Porcelain	5	0	6	11	3	4
Porcelain, burned	0	0	0	1	0	0
Creamware*	0	0	1	4	0	43
Pearlware*	0	1	0	0	1	0
Whiteware*	26	1	1	3	0	79
Yellowware*	3	0	0	0	0	5
Glass fragments						
Wine bottle	38	27	20	226	113	7
Case bottle	1	0	0	3	7	3
Tableware	18	2	0	1	12	0
Wine glass	4	0	1	0	3	0
Window glass (incomplete)	46	1	12	8	26	41
Cutlery						
Fork	2	0	0	0	0	0
Knife	1	0	0	0	0	1
Spoon, pewter	1	0	0	2	0	0
Sewing equipment						
Scissors	0	0	0	0	1	0
Utilitarian						
Hinge frag.	1	0	0	0	0	1
Tent hardware	1	0	0	0	0	0
Whetstone	0	1	0	0	0	0
Pike tip	0	0	0	0	1	1
Felling axe	0	0	0	0	1	0
Knife, clasp	0	0	1	0	0	1
Buckles, utilitarian	1	0	0	1	0	2
Personal adornment						
Buttons, metal	5	0	1	10	2	7
Buttons, wood	0	0	0	0	0	1

	Dwelling 1 (tent)	Dwelling 2 (hut)	Dwelling 3 (tent)	Dwelling 4 (tent)	Dwelling 5 (hut)	Dwelling 6 (tent)
Personal adornment (continued)						
Gold braid	0	0	0	0	2	0
Cuff links	1	0	0	0	0	1
Buckles, dress	1	0	0	0	0	0
Leather frags.	1	0	0	0	0	23
Leather heel frag.	0	0	0	0	0	1
Clothing hook	1	0	0	0	0	0
Medical supplies						
Vial frags.	3	5	4	4	5	1
Medicine bottle frags.	0	0	0	0	1	0
Coins						
British halfpenny	2	0	2	1	2	1
Spanish four real	0	0	1	0	0	0
Spanish eight real	1	0	0	0	1	0
Spanish cob	2	0	0	1	1	0
Tobacco pipes						
Stems, 3/64" bore dia.	0	0	1	0	0	0
Stems, 4/64" bore dia.	23	4	18	18	40	2
Stems, 5/64" bore dia.	3	0	2	12	31	0
Stems, 6/64" bore dia.	2	0	0	0	0	0
Unidentifiable bore	0	0	0	4	0	0
Bowl frags.	6	5	23	29	34	7
Armaments						
Musket parts	1	0	0	0	0	0
Bayonet frags.	0	0	0	1	0	0
Worms	0	0	0	0	1	0
Scabbard holder	0	0	2	0	0	0
Gunflints, British	2	1	2	1	0	5
Gunflint frags., British	2	0	6	0	0	0
Gunflints, French	0	0	1	5	2	12
Gunflint frags., French	0	0	0	4	1	0
Gunflints, burned	1	5	2	0	0	2
Musket balls	72	3	4	19	13	39
Musket balls, flattened	0	0	1	1	0	0
Musket balls w. tooth marks	1	0	0	1	0	0
Musket balls, mutilated/worked	1	0	1	0	0	1
Musket ball frags.	0	0	0	1	0	3
Lead slug	0	1	2	5	1	0
Lead shot, cut	0	0	1	0	0	0
Lead sprue	1	0	0	3	3	6
Lead slag from casting balls	10	2	28	19	9	152
Lead buckshot	9	1	11	13	8	76
Lead birdshot	0	0	2	0	0	1

*Not from the French and Indian War period.

Table 7.2

Artifacts Recovered from Other Features on Rogers Island, 1991–1998

	Storehouse (Site 1)	Latrine (Site 1)	Hospital (Site 14)	Barracks (Site 11)	Dump (Site 18)	All other sites on Rogers Island (nonfeatures)
Ceramic sherds						
Redware	7	8	2	6	12	189
Delft	98	45	4	76	117	770
Delft, burned	0	0	0	0	2	2
Buff-bodied slipware	45	2	0	5	0	36
Earthenware, burned	3	4	1	0	1	32
White salt-glazed stoneware	54	29	3	6	9	220
w. scratch blue	2	11	0	8	4	25
Gray salt-glazed stoneware	28	18	0	6	26	55
w. scratch blue	2	3	0	1	3	50
Brown stoneware	0	0	0	0	10	2
Unrefined stoneware	55	8	1	7	10	200
Unrefined stoneware, burned	1	3	1	2	0	18
Porcelain	92	7	0	6	38	77
Porcelain, burned	0	1	0	0	0	4
Creamware*	13	4	0	1	5	42
Pearlware*	0	0	0	0	1	8
Whiteware*	92	9	7	16	33	232
Whiteware, burned	0	0	0	0	0	2
Yellowware*	49	0	0	4	5	38
Glass fragments						
Wine bottle	141	178	173	137	42	1,183
Case bottle	21	0	8	0	0	77
Tableware	96	38	24	52	50	227
Wine glass	1	0	0	0	6	12
Window glass (incomplete)	146	18	14	16	0	136
Cutlery						
Fork	0	0	0	0	0	3
Knife	1	5	0	0	1	4
Spoon, pewter	0	0	2	2	0	16
Fork or spoon handle, iron	0	0	0	0	2	0
Sewing equipment						
Pins	0	4	0	0	0	2
Thimbles	1	0	0	0	0	1
Straight pin/needle frag.	0	0	0	0	1	1
Utilitarian						
Canteen frags.	0	0	0	0	0	15
Cast iron pot/kettle frag.	0	3	0	0	0	1
Hinge frag.	1	3	0	2	0	2

	Storehouse (Site 1)	Latrine (Site 1)	Hospital (Site 14)	Barracks (Site 11)	Dump (Site 18)	All other sites on Rogers Island (nonfeatures)
Utilitarian (continued)						
Tent hardware	2	6	2	0	0	4
Wheel hardware	0	34	0	0	0	2
Whetstone	2	0	0	0	0	0
Kiln furniture	0	0	0	0	0	1
Pick	0	0	0	1	0	0
Felling axe	0	2	0	1	0	0
Belt axe	0	1	0	0	0	0
Fish hooks	1	1	0	0	0	0
Lead sinker	0	0	1	0	0	1
Knife, clasp	0	0	0	0	0	3
Key	0	0	1	0	1	0
Fascine knife	0	0	1	0	0	0
Spade/shovel	0	0	1	0	0	3
Bucket	1	0	0	0	0	0
Hammer	0	0	0	0	0	3
Fireplace tongs frag.	0	0	0	0	1	0
Finial frag.	0	0	0	0	0	3
Cup frag., iron	0	0	0	0	0	1
Horseshoe	0	0	1	0	2	2
Ox shoe	0	7	0	0	0	0
Buckles, utilitarian	1	2	1	0	1	2
Personal adornment						
Buttons, metal	7	39	2	11	2	45
Buttons, wood	0	1	0	0	0	0
Buttons, bone	0	7	0	0	0	1
Buttons, glass	1	0	0	2	0	1
Cuff links	0	0	2	3	0	6
Buckles, dress	0	2	2	1	0	9
Buckle tang, brass	0	0	0	0	1	0
Clasp, copper	0	0	0	0	0	1
Leather frags.	0	0	0	0	0	4
Leather lace frags.	0	0	0	0	0	2
Leather boot heel	0	0	0	0	0	1
Tinkler	0	0	1	0	0	0
Dress pin	0	0	1	0	0	0
Medical supplies						
Vial frags.	21	73	2	17	19	168
Medicine bottle frags.	5	2	1	0	0	28
Bandage pins	0	0	2	0	0	0

	Storehouse (Site 1)	Latrine (Site 1)	Hospital (Site 14)	Barracks (Site 11)	Dump (Site 18)	All other sites on Rogers Island (nonfeatures)
Gaming items						
Clay marble	0	0	0	0	0	1
Square lead dice	0	0	0	0	0	1
Coins						
British halfpenny	2	1	1	1	0	8
Spanish one real	0	1	1	0	0	0
Spanish cob	0	0	0	1	0	1
Tobacco Pipes						
Stems, 3/64" bore dia.	0	0	0	3	0	6
Stems, 4/64" bore dia.	52	89	29	53	35	242
Stems, 5/64" bore dia.	12	9	6	4	9	163
Stems, 6/64" bore dia.	0	1	0	0	1	12
Unidentifiable bore	0	5	3	3	0	18
Bowl frags.	111	71	45	89	22	382
Armaments						
Musket parts	0	6	0	0	0	6
Bayonet frags.	1	0	0	0	0	2
Scabbard holders	0	0	0	0	0	1
Scabbard holders w. leather	0	0	0	0	0	1
Gunflints, British	6	4	3	10	0	38
Gunflint frags., British	4	4	1	7	1	17
Gunflints, French	1	6	5	5	1	13
Gunflint frags., French	1	4	4	6	2	42
Gunflints, burned	6	3	3	4	0	12
Musket balls	4	45	5	22	3	106
Musket balls, flattened	1	1	1	0	0	5
Musket balls w. tooth marks	0	0	0	0	0	20
Musket balls, mutilated/worked 1	1	1	0	0	9	
Musket ball frags.	1	1	1	2	0	3
Lead slug	1	4	1	5	1	14
Lead shot, cut	0	1	0	0	0	2
Lead sprue	0	2	0	3	1	11
Lead slag from casting balls	12	47	3	61	4	224
Lead sprig	1	0	1	0	0	0
Lead ingot	0	0	0	0	0	1
Lead buckshot	16	31	8	38	8	156
Birdshot	0	0	0	6	3	144
Bullet, lead	0	0	0	0	0	1

*Not from the French and Indian War period.

totals), 2 (ceramics), and 3 (tobacco pipes). A variety of other graphs were also prepared as we searched for patterns in each excavated feature, but they have not been included here. Admittedly, the process of interpreting each structure based upon the artifacts associated with it is only just beginning, and complete information will not be available until we publish our final technical reports. However, I am including some general observations here to give a sense of what the artifacts have revealed so far.

Ceramics

Pottery and porcelain are always the mainstay of the historical archeologist, and on Rogers Island we recovered thousands of sherds (figs. 7.1 and 7.2). Delft (tin-glazed earthenware) was clearly the most abundant ware, but stonewares were a close second, and white salt-glazed stoneware, gray salt-glazed stoneware, and the heavier unrefined stonewares were all very common. "Scratch blue" decoration appeared on many of the refined stoneware sherds, so these have been listed separately in tables 7.1 and 7.2. Other wares that were somewhat less common included redware, porcelain, buff-bodied slip-decorated earthenware, and brown stoneware. Interestingly, there were quite a few "intrusive," later sherds of creamware, pearlware, whiteware, and yellowware that were mixed into the top of each archeological site.

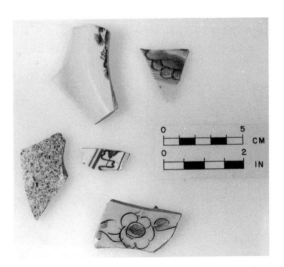

FIG. 7.1. Representative ceramics excavated on Rogers Island. *Top:* porcelain; *middle:* tin-glazed earthenware (delft); *bottom:* white salt-glazed stoneware with scratch blue decoration.

FIG. 7.2. Sherds from a chamber pot of unrefined stoneware excavated from within the soldiers' midden at Site 2.

The proportions of each ware varied considerably from site to site, and occasionally they formed patterns that may be significant. For example, redware was common only in Dwelling 3 (a tent site), whereas porcelain was most common at the storehouse (Site 1) and in the dump at Site 18. Some statistical analyses would perhaps be helpful to determine whether certain wares are consistently occurring together and to see whether certain wares correlate with other artifacts that might suggest higher (or lower) status.

Glass

Fragments of wine bottles were abundant in nearly every context and especially at Dwelling 4 (a tent site). The widespread consumption of alcohol was of course expected, as was the rather low number of fragments of square-sided case bottles. We had hoped that there might be sizable numbers of fragments from wine glasses in certain contexts, suggesting the presence of officers, but that was not the case. Wine glasses were extremely rare, and there were very small numbers of wine glass fragments in the dump at Site 18 and in Dwellings 1 and 5. We also expected tableware to correlate more with officers than with ordinary soldiers, and, once again, the dwellings with the most fragments were Dwellings 1 and 5. This certainly suggests we should look for additional types of evidence for high status (or wealth) at those two sites.

We have not yet finished counting all the fragments of window glass we recovered, and so the totals in tables 7.1 and 7.2 are not complete. However, window glass *was* found at nearly every site, in at least small quantities. The most window glass was present in the storehouse (Site 1) and in Dwelling 1, but it is still necessary to study the glass more closely before we can rule out contamination from later occupations.

Cutlery

We found a small number of bone-handled knives, two-tined forks, and pewter spoons scattered through various contexts (figs. 7.3 and 7.4), but there were not enough to make a correlation with any particular type of feature or structure.

Sewing Equipment

Sewing equipment, consisting of scissors, pins, needles, and thimbles, was universally rare, but we did find a few examples of each (figs. 7.5 and 7.6).

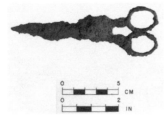

FIG. 7.3. Examples of bone-handled knives excavated from Rogers Island.

FIG. 7.4. A crumbling pewter spoon exposed on the floor of Dwelling 5.

FIG. 7.5. Scissors excavated from Dwelling 5.

FIG. 7.6. A thimble (*far right*) from the storehouse (Site 1), together with cuff links (*left*) and metal buttons (*center*) excavated on Rogers Island.

FIG. 7.7. A felling axe (before conservation) excavated from the latrine (Site 1).

FIG. 7.8. A second felling axe (before conservation) excavated from the latrine (Site 1).

Utilitarian Artifacts

Tools, architectural hardware, canteens, buckets, hardware from tents and wheels, horseshoes, and ox shoes are all represented in this broad artifact category. We did find a few examples of each of these many different artifact types, but nothing in any quantity (figs. 7.7, 7.8, 7.9, 7.10, and 7.11). Perhaps what was most surprising were the artifact types that were *not* well represented here. For example, only four fragments of cast iron pots or kettles (used for cooking) were found on the entire island, and our team found a total of only four axes, far fewer than those discovered by the Rogers Island Historical Association.

FIG. 7.9. A tin bucket excavated from one of the post molds on the perimeter of the storehouse (Site 1). It measures 8 inches tall and 8 inches in diameter.

FIG. 7.10. A pothook excavated from Dwelling 5.

FIG. 7.11. Examples of wood tent pegs excavated from underneath the dredge piles on Rogers Island.

Personal Adornment

The personal objects left behind by soldiers and officers often have a very strong impact upon those of us who study them today. After all, many soldiers probably brought only a few spartan, personal possessions with them from home, and these were things they could not easily replace if broken or lost. The sutlers in Fort Edward who sold them supplies could have replaced some wares, but often we find things that no one truly would have wanted to lose. Thus it is that when we find buttons, buckles, cuff links, or even bits of leather (which may or may not have come from clothing), we feel a stronger connection with the men as "real people" (figs. 7.6 and 7.12).

Most of the buttons that we recovered were of undecorated metal, usually brass, and we found virtually *no* numbered regimental buttons. Because numbered buttons are typical of the Revolutionary War but not of the 1750s, this certainly suggests that there was very little military occupation on the island during later years. We did find a cluster of seven bone buttons in the latrine, perhaps from an undergarment, and we found a total of thirty-nine metal buttons in the latrine, an amazing number. We also found several sets of cuff links; these were in the smallpox hospital, the barracks, and Dwelling 1.

However, there is no denying that the most interesting find came from Dwelling 5, where we discovered two strips of gold braid in 1998 (fig. 7.13). While gold braid could have found its way there for a variety of reasons, these two artifacts nevertheless became a principal reason for our believing that Dwelling 5 may have been occupied by officers.

FIG. 7.12. Examples of metal buttons and a glass inlay (*lower right*) excavated from various contexts on Rogers Island.

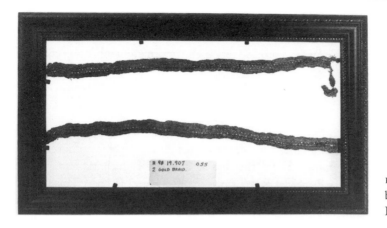

FIG. 7.13. Two strips of gold braid excavated from Dwelling 5.

Medical Supplies

A modest number of glass vial fragments—which *may* have had a medical use—were found in many different contexts on Rogers Island. However, fragments of actual medicine bottles (fig. 6.12) were extremely rare. Two bandage pins were found at the smallpox hospital, but considering the fact that many buildings served as hospitals on Rogers Island, these numbers are surprisingly low.

Coins

Both Spanish and British coins were in wide circulation in the colonies, and we did find modest numbers of British halfpennies, Spanish cobs, and Spanish minted coins on Rogers Island (figs. 7.14 and 7.15). We did not find them with the frequency enjoyed by Earl Stott and the Rogers Island Historical Association, and I admit to being amazed at their discovery of literally hundreds of coins during their thirty years of digging. All the same, we did find coins that had been lost on the floors of dwellings, in the storehouse, in the latrine, in the smallpox hospital, in the barracks, and elsewhere. I believe

FIG. 7.14. A Spanish silver real, dated 1751 and minted in Mexico City, excavated from the smallpox hospital (Site 14).

FIG. 7.15. The obverse and reverse of a piece of Spanish cob money found in Dwelling 1. Drawing by Ellen Pawelczak.

we all experience a bit of a thrill upon discovering an early coin—partially because we feel a connection to the individual who lost it—but for an archeologist coins also provide very useful information for dating cultural layers.

Tobacco Pipes

Fragments of tobacco pipes were abundant in nearly all contexts on Rogers Island, and bores typically measured either $\frac{4}{64}$ or $\frac{5}{64}$ of an inch, which is very appropriate for the middle and late eighteenth century. A modest number displayed maker's marks; "R. Tippet" (Robert Tippet or Tippett) was the most common mark. The Tippet family in Bristol, England, were important pipe makers from about 1660 until 1720, and other pipe makers continued to manufacture pipes bearing the Tippet mark after that. Few were complete (fig. 7.16), and most showed signs of use, that is, staining on the inside of the bowl. Pipes were found in virtually all the excavated dwellings, and they were especially common in the storehouse (Site 1) and the barracks. If archeology is any indication, then smoking was probably the favorite leisure activity on Rogers Island!

Armaments

In that Rogers Island was a military encampment, we expected evidence of armaments to be common in all contexts, and that was definitely the case. We did not find examples of the more "glamorous" artifacts, such as swords, muskets, cannons, or even cannonballs, but we did not expect that. Rather, musket balls, gunflints, birdshot, and buckshot were common just about everywhere, and we found bits of melted lead slag and sprue everywhere we dug (figs. 7.17 and 7.18). Clearly the soldiers spent much time melting lead to make their own balls, and we often found spots where the sand on

FIG. 7.16. A complete tobacco pipe bowl lying on the floor of Dwelling 5.

FIG. 7.17. Examples of lead sprue, demonstrating how musket balls were detached from the sprue.

FIG. 7.18. Examples of lead discovered on Rogers Island, including musket balls, shot, and slag.

FIG. 7.19. A bayonet fragment excavated from Dwelling 5.

Rogers Island had been burned to a bright red. In looking more closely at those spots, we would then find small bits of melted lead and balls mixed into the sand.

We were especially curious as to whether gunflints would more commonly be British or French, because French gunflints were considered to be of superior quality in the eighteenth century. Ironically, after our several years of digging, there was no significant difference in frequency. When we added both whole and fragmentary gunflints together, there were 114 British gunflints and 115 French. We also found very small numbers of musket parts, a few scabbard holders, and a single "worm," but these were all surprisingly rare. Even bayonets were represented by only four fragments (fig. 7.19).

Food

Historical sources describe a wide variety of foods eaten by the army residing on Rogers Island. Just one source, Jabez Fitch, Jr., describes eating corn, rice, "chocalet," fig "pudden," eggs, "chees," butter, "suger," cake, "huccle berrys," "rass berrys," "black berrys," plums, apples, "rheubarb," and more. He also drank "rhum," "cherry rhum," grog, wine, "sider," "bear," and a "Dram of Cherry." Unfortunately, most of these foods leave no traces archeologically.

On the other hand, soldiers' diaries describe several types of meat that were eaten, and butchered bones *do* leave a tangible record in the ground. Fitch made only a few references to animals at the encampment in Fort Edward, and these included "This Day I Se 48 oxen Swim over ye River" (June 8, 1757); "Toard Night there Came In an Ox from Ft Wm Henry" (August 8, 1757); "I went Over to ye Island and Took ye Charge of 35 Cattle & Brought them over ye River and Bated them on ye Plain all Day" (August 18, 1757); and "at Night Chappel & I Bought Som Fresh Fish" (August 20, 1757). These references to cattle and fish certainly do not provide a quantitative sense of what was being consumed, nor do they give a sense of how much meat came from domesticated versus wild animals, nor how much meat was fresh versus salted. Still, they give archeologists a sense of what to look for on Rogers Island.

Our excavations have recovered many thousands of butchered animal bones, from every possible context on Rogers Island, and Jene Romeo has been identifying these as part of her dissertation at the City University of New York. Thus far, the sample she has been examining includes 54,046 bones and bone fragments, and these were found in historic middens, trash pits, a latrine, underfoot on the floors of huts and around fireplaces, and even inside postholes. Some of the bones also derive from prehistoric contexts, including firepits, trash pits, and middens, and these bones were predominantly deer. It is not yet possible to provide quantitative data, but the final faunal analysis and interpretation of foodways will soon be available in Romeo's dissertation.

A preliminary review of her results indicates that within military contexts, cow and pig bones were most frequent among domesticated animals, followed by sheep, whereas wild animals included some deer, fish, and rabbit. Fishing was no doubt common in the Hudson River, and historical sources suggest a great deal of fishing. Still, the extremely acidic soil on Rogers Island has resulted in very poor preservation conditions, and only modest numbers of fish vertebrae, the most durable part of a fish, have been discovered. It will never be possible to quantify the importance of fish in the soldiers' diet.

The archeological record indicates that the vast majority of what was being consumed by the military came from domesticated animals, and while there were great numbers of pig bones, there is no question that cattle contributed a higher percentage of meat to the diet. Many of the bones were sawn, but many others had been chopped or cut. Typically butchers

FIG. 7.20. A complete pig skull lying within the soldiers' midden at Site 2.

would have accompanied the troops on their expeditions, and a butcher would have killed the fresh animals and chopped them up. Curiously enough, several nearly complete pig skulls were discovered at various sites on Rogers Island (including ones next to Dwelling 1 and inside Dwelling 3) (figs. 5.16 and 7.20), but there were no cow skulls. One possibility that Jene Romeo has pointed out to me is that military suppliers sometimes included pig skulls in the brine inside barrels of salted pork, and it may be that soldiers simply threw these out when encountered—the skulls really had no meat value.

Throughout the excavations of the 1990s, we discovered only one animal burial—obviously not a source of food—and it was that of a dog, found on the eastern edge of Dwelling 5, the so-called "Officers' House" (fig. 7.21). The animal's skeleton was complete and in a reasonably good state of preservation, and its body lay east-west with its head at the eastern end of the burial pit. It was relatively small, and no data are available as to what breed it might have been. No artifacts were found in association with it, so it is impossible to state definitively that the dog dated to the French and Indian War period (rather than being a later intrusion).

FIG. 7.21. The dog burial discovered at Dwelling 5.

Chapter 8

Archeology at Other Military Sites in Fort Edward

WHILE THE ARCHEOLOGICAL research conducted on Rogers Island has certainly been the most intensive ever done in Fort Edward, there have been several other excavations in that community that have exposed significant remains from the period of the French and Indian War or the American Revolution.

Archeology Underneath Broadway

Just before the construction of the modern sewage treatment plant on Little Wood Creek, an archeological consulting firm, Collamer & Associates, Inc., was employed in 1986 by Clough, Harbour & Associates to dig trenches into the outer earthworks of Fort Edward and under several of the streets in the modern village. Jeanette Collamer and her associates discovered sizable numbers of military artifacts underneath Broadway, the main street in Fort Edward, where British lines had extended north from the fort. I worked as a consultant on that project for a few days in 1986 and was extremely impressed by the richness of artifacts and features underneath that busy thoroughfare. Unfortunately, none of this work has been published upon.

The Outworks for the Original Fort Edward

During the work by Joel Grossman of Grossman and Associates at the Little Wood Creek site in the late 1980s (fig. 8.1), his extensive archeological dig found a dark stain from an outer fortification line of eighteenth-century Fort Edward (fig. 8.2). Grossman referred to this as a "spear point shaped form of a military bastion or outwork" in the northwest corner of his project site. A thin layer of what was probably decomposed wood at the base of each trench suggested that this outwork was constructed of earth, and it may have functioned as a "firing or defensive position." Only six small

FIG. 8.1. The Little Wood Creek site during excavation. Courtesy of the Rogers Island Visitors Center.

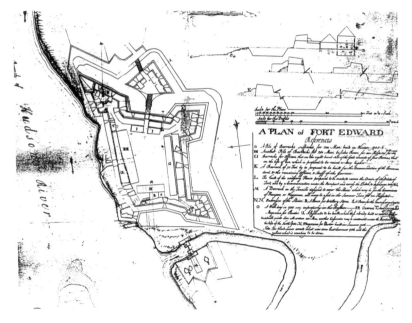

FIG. 8.2. "A Plan of Fort Edward" in 1756. Crown Collection of Photographs of American Maps, New York State Library.

trenches were excavated here, and Grossman recovered 402 artifacts, including ceramics, pipes, and a British farthing dating to 1746.

Archeology at the Fort in Fort Edward

The fort that the British began to build in Fort Edward in 1757 has seen very little archeological research compared with other colonial forts. The only

FIG. 8.3. The 1995 excavation into one of the lawns atop historic Fort Edward. Facing east.

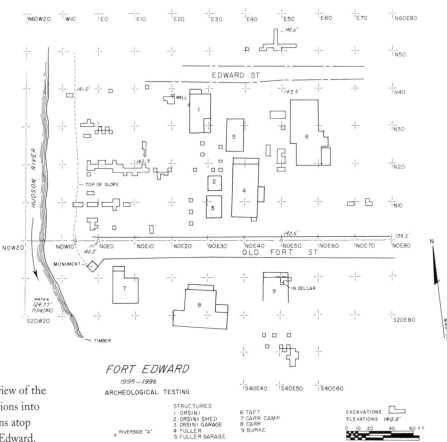

FIG. 8.4. A plan view of the 1995–1996 excavations into several of the lawns atop the original Fort Edward.

Prepared by Gordon De Angelo.

professional archeology ever undertaken at the site of Fort Edward was in 1995, 1996, 2002, and 2003 as teams from Adirondack Community College (ACC) under my direction dug pits and trenches throughout several of the lawns that cover the fort (figs. 8.3 and 8.4). These excavations found enough charred timbers to define both the eastern and western edges of the fort, including the approximate locations of both the East and West Barracks.

In 1995, a small amount of digging was conducted inside the dry moat that surrounded the fort. This originally measured from 25 to 60 feet wide and 10 to 15 feet deep. Intensive digging then followed inside the East Casemate room, a well-protected room under the ramparts on the east side of the fort. Typically, casemate rooms provided ample protection during any bombardment, and charred logs or beams have survived at different levels, running to a total depth of about 7 feet through what is now fine, shifting sand. Some of these beams were 8 inches square, and the bottom floor of the casemate room was about 8 feet deep.

On the western side of the fort, alongside the Hudson River, the field school from ACC discovered destroyed fireplaces and intact wood beams running north-south parallel to the river and only several feet from the river's edge (fig. 8.5). These extended for over 125 feet, with pockets of artifacts buried alongside. The finds included deep ash concentrations and timbers, Spanish cob money, and clusters of musket balls and lead sprue, and everywhere there were stains from ditches and post molds. The longest stains, running east-west, lined up with the sally port that is known to have run to the river on the western side of the fort. There also were three destroyed fireplaces in a row, running north-south down the western side of

FIG. 8.5. Excavations along the riverbank between Fort Edward and the Hudson River. Facing southeast.

the fort, each 34 feet from the next one. These fireplaces had probably run down the center of the West Barracks.

In 1996 we extended our excavations into the front and rear lawns of a house that lies atop the southeast corner of the fort. In the 1960s the owner of the house had discovered beams from the fort in his cellar, at a depth of about 6 feet below grade, so the house clearly straddled a deep casemate room. New excavations in the cellar reexposed beams running east-west, along with a corner of the casemate constructed with a mortise and tenon joint, as well as additional beams that were running north-south (fig. 8.6). The wood was very soft and punky, and the timbers were about 15 inches wide. In the front yard of the same house, the casemate continued to run north, with the wood ranging from 3 to 7 feet in depth. The interior of this room was filled with extremely loose sand that required shoring as the walls constantly collapsed. At the bottom, 6 feet below the present ground surface, we discovered wood, spikes, a flattened musket ball, and a layer of boards that almost certainly had been the floor of the casemate room.

In 2002 and 2003, we returned to the fort to do some additional testing in a yard that lies on the south side of Old Fort Street, next to the commemorative stone marker at the west end of that street. This yard had not

FIG. 8.6. Wood beams from the original Fort Edward, exposed in a cellar on Old Fort Street.

FIG. 8.7. Drawing a soil profile in 2002 inside a casemate room or cellar, part of the original Fort Edward. Facing northeast.

been available to us during our earlier work, and while our new finds included more prehistoric than historic artifacts (see chapter 1), we nevertheless did find a deep casemate room or cellar on the very edge of the street (fig. 8.7). Even more exciting was the discovery of a sheep metapodial that the soldiers had reworked into a whistle or flute (fig. 8.8).

More archeology within the ruins of Fort Edward would no doubt be productive, as very little of the fort's outline has yet been verified. From our preliminary testing, it is quite extraordinary that so much has survived below ground from virtually the largest British fort of the French and Indian War. Perhaps in time it will be possible to remove the existing houses from atop old Fort Edward and to use archeology to help the fort site become the major attraction that it deserves to be.

Providing Supplies to the Soldiers

Beginning in 2001, the main focus of our most recent work in Fort Edward has been a sutler's house, or storehouse, on the east bank of the Hudson River where one or more sutlers sold supplies to the army (fig. 8.2). There are historical references to a brewery and ovens that were also located there in the late 1750s, as well as a barracks. This wooded lot is located just south of the ruins of the original Fort Edward and directly across from the soldiers' and rangers' huts on Rogers Island. The sutler's area is approximately one hundred feet east of the river's edge, and its surface lies about ten feet above the current level of the Hudson River (fig. 8.9).

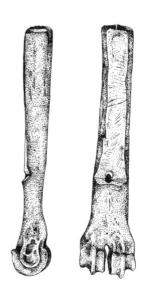

FIG. 8.8. A bone whistle or flute found inside the ruins of the original Fort Edward. It measures 4⅜" long. Drawn by Ellen Pawelczak.

FIG. 8.9. The wooded sut-
ler's area alongside the
Hudson River, showing
excavation pits in 2002.
Facing southeast.

In the mid-1990s, the site was assaulted by treasure hunters who arrived
by boat and crept into the woods, where they left many deep craters across
the surface of the property. As a result, in 1995 and 1996, when our field
school was digging nearby atop the site of Fort Edward, we often wondered
whether anything remained of the 1750s occupation at what we began referring to as the "sutler's site." Fragments of wine bottles and other artifacts
sometimes appeared in the backdirt of looters, but at that time we did not
know whether the site had been completely destroyed or whether only the
surface had been disturbed.

In the summer of 2001 I sent a small crew to excavate inside one of the
largest of the looters' holes to find out how deep and intact the site might
be. Without knowing it, our team dropped down into the cellar of what
had been a large structure, and we discovered that the main 1750s occupation extended to a depth of over 2 meters. Seven or 8 square meters were
excavated to this level. We were delighted to find that the lowest layers of
the site were intact and contained two large scatters of bricks, 1,860 fragments of wine bottles (including one with the initials "Gd" on it), two strap
hinges, mid-eighteenth-century coins, and even the metal edge of a spade.
The looters' holes had only just scraped the surface of the main occupation
layer, and we found the site to be the deepest and most intact of any known
French and Indian War site in Fort Edward. In 2001, given the depth of
deposits, it was not possible to reach sterile soil in any of the test pits, so we
filled in the excavation with hay bales and resolved to return in 2002. Iron-

ically, even the looters' own artifacts were interesting: we found two ther-
mos bottles, one labeled with the name "Lassie," the other with the "Dukes
of Hazzard," and one of them was still full of coffee!

In the summer of 2002 we expanded our work at the sutler's site and
exposed wood and stains along the eastern wall and at the southeastern
corner of the foundation. Because of the depth of the remains, a lot of
wood had survived from this structure, and the two scatters of bricks found
in 2001 suggest that nogging walls—a timber frame filled with brick-
work—may have lined the interior of the cellar. And all across the cellar
floor, we found wonderful things. In fact, we did not dare announce anything to the press for fear that collectors might attempt to finish what we
had started.

But a new question arose. Was this just a short-term sutler's house or
storehouse in the 1750s, or did the deep cellar and substantial construction
indicate a building that had stood for much longer? This is the most substantial, best-preserved building we have *ever* found in Fort Edward after
twelve years of digging ephemeral military sites. Yet there was one historic
occupation in Fort Edward that we know predated 1755. That was the trading post and warehouses of the Dutch fur trader John Henry Lydius, who
traded with Indians over a huge area in upstate New York and Canada
beginning in 1731. When the British fort began to go up in 1755, we know
that Fort Edward was very close to Lydius's trading post.

Fort Edward town and village historian R. Paul McCarty, using historical sources, is absolutely convinced that our so-called sutler's house is one
of Lydius's earlier buildings, perhaps a storehouse that continued to be used
after the British sutler(s) arrived. If so, this building would have been used
for a twenty- or thirty-year period, from the 1730s until the 1750s or 1760s.

We have dug only 5 or 10 percent of this foundation down to sterile soil,
and we have focused on exposing and following the stains, the outline of
the building. We now know that it measured 12 feet wide by about 45 feet
long. We have found 9 strap hinges, in pairs, around the half-exposed
perimeter, suggesting at least five outside doors. On the cellar floor we
have recovered very sizable quantities of sherds of delft, white salt-glazed
stoneware, and some porcelain. We have found several shoe buckles, a
mouth harp, a fork, 2 knives, a pewter spoon, 2 barrel hoops, 19 metal buttons, 877 rosehead nails and spikes, a lot of window glass, a complete bayonet, a nearly complete wine glass with an air-twist stem (fig. 8.10), 6 or 7
Spanish and British coins (fig. 8.11), a French liard (a copper coin with the
likeness of Louis XIV) dating to 1695, 16 musket balls, 4 British gunflints,
and 2 French gunflints.

There were unused tobacco pipes everywhere—a total of 974 fragments,
including a cluster of at least 25 pipes that I discovered in the wall of a pit
after 5:00 P.M. on the last day of our dig in 2002 (fig. 8.12). I literally had to

FIG. 8.10. An elegant wine glass stem discovered inside the sutler's house in 2002.

FIG. 8.12. A cache of unused tobacco pipes discovered at the sutler's house in 2002.

FIG. 8.11. Some of the Spanish silver coins found inside the sutler's house.

burrow into the wall of the next test pit to get the pipes out at the last minute. Later, I found that the supervisor at the sutler's site, Matt Rozell, had identified me on the artifact bag as "Dr. Woodchuck"! Several different maker's marks were represented within this cache of unused pipes, but they were chiefly "RT" (Robert Tippet) pipes (also see the frontispiece).

After the close of the 2002 excavations, the count of wine bottle fragments is now up to 3,456, some of which still have wires wrapped around the neck to hold the cork in. In 1759, General Amherst ordered that a brewery be constructed upon the site of the old sutler's house, for brewing spruce beer, and that may very well be the source of many of the wine bottles we found.

There is no body of literature that deals with the architecture or contents of sutlers' houses during the French and Indian War, and I am not aware of anything published by archeologists on this topic. This makes it hard to make comparisons with other sites, but if we assume that soldiers bought from sutlers the things they could not obtain as standard army issue, then the great quantities of wine bottles and unused tobacco pipes would suggest a lively trade in the "vices" that soldiers loved to have! The many sets of door hinges may well favor a storehouse type of building, with many entranceways, and the several coins found in quite a small area may suggest that there was lots of buying and selling going on. We do not know yet whether this structure began its life as one of Lydius's buildings, but it certainly underwent intensive use in the 1750s.

The Scientific Investigation of Jane McCrea

Anyone familiar with Fort Edward's history knows the story of the most famous person who lived and died in that community: It was Jane McCrea, a young Scottish-Presbyterian woman, a minister's daughter, who was murdered and scalped in Fort Edward during the early stages of the American Revolution in 1777 (fig. 8.13). Her murder occurred while she was being escorted by Indians to General John Burgoyne's camp, shortly before his disastrous defeat at the Battle of Saratoga. Jane McCrea was subsequently buried and reburied on three separate occasions. During the years that we have dug in Fort Edward, we have repeatedly heard her story, or stories, because they are all different—different stories about how she died, about how old she was, what color her hair was, and whether or not she had been

FIG. 8.13. Jane McCrea. Courtesy of Chapman Historical Museum.

FIG. 8.14. The entrance to Union Cemetery in Fort Edward, site of the graves of Jane McCrea and Duncan Campbell.

pretty. Her final resting spot has been a popular tourist destination for many years, but visitors have known very little about who she really was (fig. 8.14).

Jane McCrea was probably born in early 1754, and she was perhaps typical in that she came from a family split into both Loyalist and Patriot factions. Her fiancé, David Jones, was a Loyalist with John Burgoyne's army, and she waited for David as the British moved south from Canada in the summer of 1777. Jane stayed behind in Fort Edward as other settlers fled for Albany, and she does not appear to have believed herself to be in any danger. The home where she was staying was that of Sara McNeil, an older, robust woman of about fifty-five. Sara had earlier come to the colonies to retrieve the body of Major Duncan Campbell of Inverawe, an officer of the Scottish Black Watch who had been mortally wounded nineteen years earlier while serving under General Abercrombie at the siege of Fort Ticonderoga. Sara McNeil was also a cousin to General Simon Fraser, a leading British general with Burgoyne's army, so she too believed herself to be safe as British forces approached.

Some of the Indians attached to Burgoyne's army entered the McNeil house on July 27 and dragged both women out by their hair, along with a young man, Norman Morrison. Jane was then placed on a horse and led up the hill toward where the Fort Edward High School now stands, while the other two were forced to walk to the British camp. Unfortunately, Jane never made it. Or more specifically, only her hair made it, because her scalp was recognized in a pile of scalps that was turned in for bounties at Burgoyne's camp. Her fiancé, David, recovered her body, and she was subsequently buried a few miles south of the village of Fort Edward.

The specifics of how she died were disputed at the time, and the controversy continues even today. The British version was that two Indian leaders had fought over Jane, and she was killed in the process. The Indians, on the other hand, maintained that a musket ball fired from the direction of Fort Edward had felled her from the horse, after which they did remove her scalp. In the days that followed, Jane's murder provoked a huge backlash among the colonial population. Thousands signed up to fight against the British, and Jane's death is often credited as a principal factor behind the overwhelming American victory at Saratoga on October 10. Although she herself was a victim, her bloody demise helped defeat Burgoyne. David Jones reportedly then deserted, moved to Canada, and never married. Local mythology holds that he "never smiled again."

But Jane was not to rest in peace. In 1822, her body was exhumed, and she was transported to State Street Cemetery in Fort Edward, where oral tradition states that her coffin was laid on top of the brick-lined vault of her old companion, Sara McNeil. Sara had outlasted Jane by twenty-two years, passing away in 1799. The two coffins rested on top of each other until 1852, at which time the Champlain Canal removed a portion of State Street Cemetery. Jane's body—reduced now to bones—was moved again, and came to rest in Union Cemetery, where a prominent limestone monument was erected atop her remains, paid for by her niece, Sarah Hanna Payne (fig. 8.15). A cast iron fence was placed around her, and the gravestone of

FIG. 8.15. The Jane McCrea limestone monument in Union Cemetery, erected in 1852.

Duncan Campbell was later moved inside the fence alongside hers. A disturbing story from 1852 states that some of the "leading citizens" of Fort Edward arrived to each take one of her bones as a souvenir, and that a "Dr. Sanford of New York," owner of Long Island in Lake George, took her skull and then kept it on a shelf in a cabinet.

But the story does not end there. With each passing generation, the legend of Jane McCrea grew stronger, and she became more beautiful; dozens of paintings have depicted her, two Indians, and sometimes the horse. Perhaps the most famous painting is the one by John Vanderlyn in the collections of the Wadsworth Atheneum Museum of Art in Hartford, Connecticut, in which Jane is shown cowering on her knees, with one Indian clutching her long hair and another about to plant a tomahawk in her skull. Jane is always very beautiful, looking sad and helpless, and the Indians are typically drawn with features that are positively demonic. Ironically, the few historical descriptions of Jane's appearance suggest that she was extremely plain and may have been somewhat "discolored" around the eyes. Chances are that her family would not recognize her in the adoring portraits that commemorate her memory!

Earlier generations of Americans were typically instructed about Jane in school, but today it appears that only New York State schoolchildren, Revolutionary War historians, and reenactors are familiar with her story. While she continues to be a local icon, she has been forgotten elsewhere. It was in February of 2002 that I listened to Fort Edward's two leading historians, Paul McCarty and Eileen Hannay, discussing Jane for the umpteenth time. They described how an elderly relative, in fact the oldest-known surviving relative, had written to them for about twenty years. Mrs. Mary McCrea Deeter, aged ninety-seven, bemoaned how Jane had slipped from view and wondered what could be done to restore her to prominence.

I wrote to Mrs. Deeter and asked if she would consider a modern forensic study that would establish whether it was, in fact, Jane McCrea's bones that lay buried in Union Cemetery. We also hoped that getting the story out would help us to locate some of the bones that had apparently been taken in 1852. These two points were critical in getting a court order: the family's right to know, and the importance of restoring the skeleton to an intact state.

Mrs. Deeter immediately wrote back to me, enthusiastically supporting the forensic work, and promising a lock of her hair, her daughter's hair, and even her grandson's hair for DNA testing. With the family's excited support, I retained attorney William Nikas, the former owner of Rogers Island, and a petition was drafted in the summer of 2002 that was signed by Mrs. Deeter. I placed this petition in the *Glens Falls Post-Star* as a legal advertisement, and after thirty days went by, the Supreme Court in Washington County ruled in November that we would be allowed to proceed

FIG. 8.16. The Jane McCrea monument as it was hoisted from her grave site by Glen Ward of Ward Memorials.

with the exhumation. This had to be postponed until the spring of 2003 because Union Cemetery was closed for the winter.

Finally, on April 9, 2003, our team of scientists converged upon Union Cemetery at 6:00 A.M., and by 8:30 P.M. we were done with our investigation. During that fourteen-hour period, we moved the monument off the grave (fig. 8.16), installed a tent over and around the grave, excavated and sifted the sand from a large trench, exposed the original burial trench, discovered the remains of a box containing human bones, removed these, measured and identified the bones, x-rayed them on-site, removed four bone samples with a saw in order to conduct DNA testing, held a Presbyterian burial service—conducted by the Reverend John Barclay of the First Presbyterian Church in Glens Falls—placed the bones within a new coffin (a plain pine box), returned the box to the bottom of the burial trench, and completely backfilled the excavation trench. It was a *very* long day!

We had at least two dozen staff on site, the result of fourteen months of preparations, many hundreds of hours of planning, hundreds of phone calls and emails, and many letters. But our plan from the beginning had been to conduct all the work on-site, with complete reburial of all remains at the end of the day. We did not want to be accused of scattering the remains of Jane McCrea to laboratories all over the country, from which her bones might never return. The forensic scientists were headed by Lowell Levine of the New York State Police Forensics Investigation Center in Albany, and accompanied by his wife Kathryn, a hair and fiber expert; Anthony Folsetti, head of the C. A. Pound Laboratory at the University of Florida in Gainesville; and Herbert Buckley, head of forensic imaging for the New York State Police.

FIG. 8.17. Part of the scientific team that conducted "The Scientific Investigation of Jane McCrea" on April 9, 2003. The tent that surrounded the grave site is on the right.

The scientists were there to conduct a complete skeletal exam of the remains of Jane McCrea and to do a computerized facial reconstruction, if possible. They were accompanied by Ben Williams, the grandson of Mrs. Deeter; and our archeological team, with John Farrell and Matt Rozell doing nearly all of the digging. Several archeological volunteers sifted all the dirt from the grave, and they included Linda White, Roland Smith, Gerd Sommer, Mary Doeden, Paula Dennis, and others (fig. 8.17). Additional support was provided by cemetery staff, funeral home staff, attorney William Nikas, and others. In late afternoon our radiologist dashed onto the site with his portable x-ray unit, returning with the developed x-rays just an hour later. And this was done in the snow in thirty-degree temperatures. We were accompanied by state police and county deputies because of the possibility of protesters—and we did *not* want protesters to turn this investigation into a circus.

That was a very real possibility because, beginning in November of 2002, we had been subjected to many salacious letters to the editor in the local newspaper, the *Glens Falls Post-Star*, and a petition had been circulated locally that opposed the exhumation. In the process, we discovered that myths about Jane McCrea were multiplying, some incredible distortions were being told about her history, and the village mayor was telling the newspaper that Fort Edward would "lose its history" if we were allowed to proceed. The Fort Edward Village Board even passed a resolution against the exhumation (although the burial site was not within the village). A local columnist for the *Glens Falls Post-Star*—known as the "North Country Curmudgeon"—accused me and attorney Nikas of being "ghouls." And in perhaps the strangest twist, I was told that some local McCreas had become uncomfortable and were asking, "What if [the scientists] discover that she was black?" It had all become somewhat irrational.

In a series of editorials and articles, the *Glens Falls Post-Star* came out solidly in favor of our research, and this reflected the community's overwhelming support for the project. A host of local historians, archeologists, businesspeople, and town leaders were all very excited at the prospect of replacing myths about Jane McCrea with at least a few "facts." Two protesters *did* make an appearance at the cemetery on April 9, and the sheriff's deputies chased them out. (The same two protesters had previously tried to get a court order to dig up Major Robert Rogers in New Hampshire, in order to turn his remains into a tourist attraction in Fort Edward—see chapter 2.)

Our work in Union Cemetery was the first of its kind in the Fort Edward area, in effect a detailed forensic examination of a significant historic personage. After our tent was erected around the grave site, we laid out an excavation trench that ran east-west from where the monument had stood. John Farrell commenced shoveling out the soft sand, and buckets of sand were carried outside the tent to where we had sifters on top of tarpaulins. John shoveled about two vertical feet of sand, and then Matt Rozell shoveled the next two feet or so. It was while Matt was digging that the dark outline of an east-west burial trench began to appear, 20 inches wide (north-south). They extended the excavation trench farther to the east so as to get *all* of the burial trench exposed.

After a while, with only a few bits of wood/charcoal coming up, we began to feel a little discouraged. Attorney Nikas and I stood on the south side of the burial trench, agreeing that this was becoming a bit like Geraldo Rivera opening up Al Capone's vault, only to find nothing inside! But two or three minutes later, Matt carefully exposed the top of a human cranium. I then became the digger in the bottom of the trench, assisted by Matt, and I proceeded with trowel, brushes, and delicate wooden tools (fig. 8.18). Everything that took place in the grave was recorded with Matt's video camera, and it totaled about seven hours of footage.

The digging inside the trench was easy because it was fine sand, but hard because all the bones were wedged very tightly together inside what had formerly been a 20-inch (north-south) by 24-inch (east-west) box. The box was gone, and only staining marked its former outline. As I brushed and extracted the bones, the forensic scientists hovered above, waiting for bones they could identify and measure. Mrs. Deeter's grandson stood at the west end of the excavation trench, taking notes, and Matt Rozell stood just to the west, taking bones from me and passing them up to the scientists above. The doctors had set up a folding table at the southeast corner of the

FIG. 8.18. The author working inside the grave of Jane McCrea on April 9, 2003. Courtesy of Ed O'Dell.

tent, and it was there where Tony Folsetti cleaned sand off the bones and inventoried, measured, and photographed them. Also, at the end of the afternoon, it was Tony who used the saw to collect the DNA samples.

When I first saw the top of the cranium, in the southeast corner of its former box, it was upright and looked very solid and intact. I admit that that was *not* what I wanted! I did *not* see any marks from scalping on the frontal bone, and the sutures were very "closed"—it was a very mature-looking skull. There were disintegrating bone fragments around it, and as I troweled and brushed, I would occasionally encounter little coffin nails in the ground. There were about two dozen coffin nails forming an outline for where the box had once been, but the wood had completely disintegrated in the acid soil.

At the start of the exhumation, I passed up several fragmentary bones to the forensic team, but I focused on trying to get the skull out. I then found the mandibles wedged against one side of the skull, upside down, and I turned these over. *All* the teeth were missing, and bone regrowth was occurring all along the length of the jaws. This was an *old* individual! I did not say anything to the others, but I knew that the skull and mandibles could not be from Jane McCrea. As I then worked to extricate the long bones, Lowell Levine called down to ask if I could come up for a minute. He was smiling as he said, "There are *two* individuals here!" That was a surprise. But soon, as more bones were lifted out, I realized that he was surely right, because there were just too many of everything! One individual was larger and older than the other, and both appeared to be women. Both pelvises were there, and I noticed that the epiphyses were falling off the ends of a humerus, so one woman was definitely quite young, and her pelvis was quite gracile. The cancellous bones, the ribs and vertebrae, were in terrible shape—very decayed—and many of these bones were missing. There were just a small number of ankle and foot bones present.

There were no artifacts inside where the coffin box had been, except for the coffin nails, and there were no traces of hair or fabric. The thickness of the deposit (the box and its contents) was no more than 8 to 9 inches, and I troweled underneath the bones until I could see nothing but gray sand. The project photographer, Ed O'Dell, was shooting the remains with three cameras, and we were working quickly because the family did not want our work at the grave to extend into a second day. The question immediately arose, Who was the second woman? If the "young" woman was a very slightly built Jane McCrea, then who was the older woman?

The likely choice is, of course, Sara McNeil, the robust woman captured with Jane in 1777. Sara was born in 1722, so she was fifty-five when the two women were captured, and she had one daughter, grandchildren, and a long line of descendants down to the present day. While I was still in the bottom of the trench, the scientists asked me how old Sara had been at death, so I called Eileen Hannay on my cell phone. The immediate response was that Sara did not die until 1799, so she was seventy-seven when we know she was buried in State Street Cemetery. I relayed this to the doctors, who were delighted because the "older woman" with nearly closed sutures could easily have been that old. Since Jane had been buried *on top of* Sara in the previous cemetery, it appears that the two were moved together when the Champlain Canal came through in 1852, at which time both women were buried in the same box, Jane for her third burial and Sara for her second.

Ironically, there was no historical record that Sara had ever been moved, there was no stone to commemorate her remains, and the community had always assumed she was still in the prior cemetery. So, subject to our DNA testing (and comparisons with modern relatives and descendants), it appears that the two women who were immortalized in the same murder story have now come to share the same grave forever. Ironically, it was the young, murdered woman, Jane, who has been remembered throughout history, whereas the older woman, who had a lifetime of accomplishments in the community, has been largely forgotten. Sara McNeil has several known descendants in the Fort Edward area, so we are now eager to finally give her a measure of recognition. The skeleton of the young woman, presumably Jane McCrea, is missing its skull, as well as some of the bones from the right-hand side of her body, and we believe this confirms the stories about her bones having been taken as souvenirs in 1852.

Mrs. Deeter's original request was that Jane McCrea be brought back into popular consciousness, and we have tried very hard to do that, while trying to do this in as respectful a manner as possible. Hopefully one of the outcomes of our work will be to tell a much more interesting story about women's lives here on the frontier of colonial New York. Sara and Jane will now be linked forever, both Scottish-Presbyterian, one petite, young, and tragically murdered and the other stocky, long-lived, and perhaps much more representative of women in the community.

Chapter 9

Conclusions, Future Work, and What to See in Fort Edward

QUITE A FEW archeological sites have survived from the French and Indian War, although very few have the integrity of Rogers Island. This is a very intact military site, and it has very little contamination, even from the Revolutionary War period. Prior to our own work, Earl Stott and his enthusiastic friends conducted excavations on the island for almost thirty years, exposing many fireplaces and huts. Unfortunately, little survives from their work that can be seen or studied. Today we cannot view the fireplaces, few artifacts are still in Fort Edward, there are no usable measured drawings, but there *is* a huge body of folklore. For example, the impression was created during Stott's work that human bones were found just about everywhere on Rogers Island, yet the only human bones that our project encountered were from a Native American, along with a few finger bones inside a posthole.

Originally there would have been huts and tents covering large areas on Rogers Island in the 1750s, typically in long rows and also probably in between the massive barracks buildings. In the 1990s our team of professional and avocational archeologists excavated and recorded the remains of huts, tents, dumps, a storehouse, a latrine, a hospital, and at least one barracks building. Unlike our predecessors who dug on the island, we chose to leave all fireplaces intact so they could be appreciated by future generations. We also found prehistoric Native American sites covering much of Rogers Island, and there were sizable prehistoric camps both at Site 1 (underlying the storehouse) and at Site 14 (underlying the smallpox hospital). This prehistoric component is a very critical part of the island's story, and it is fully as significant as the history of the soldiers and officers who lived there.

We exposed fragmentary remains from many badly disturbed structures, but in making a systematic comparison of the six best-preserved dwelling sites, our team has discovered that huts and tents varied in the quality of construction, in size, probably in permanency, and in artifact quantities and ratios. Some of this variance in quality and contents was no doubt the result of soldiers who remained in residence throughout the fall and winter and were not fortunate enough to be able to go home after a summer campaign. Still, the rank of the occupants would also have helped to determine the quality of a structure and its contents. The six dwellings that I singled out for discussion range all the way from very ephemeral tents up to very substantial huts. In quality of construction, it is hard to imagine Dwellings 2 and 5 as anything less than officers' residences, although this is hard to prove.

Of our many finds, unquestionably our most significant discovery was made by Matthew Rozell, who led the team that carefully exposed the outline of the smallpox hospital at the southern end of Rogers Island. This is the very first such hospital ever dug at an eighteenth-century military encampment in the United States. Because Rogers Island functioned for much of its history as a giant hospital complex, the uncovering of this grim and elusive site was especially satisfying. We were able to expose some of the posts that outlined this temporary structure, as well as the palisade walls on two sides of it, yet it presents us with a lingering mystery because no pottery has survived at this site. Were all the dishes thrown out after each feeding of the dying soldiers?

In reviewing the thousands of artifacts unearthed over the years, we have learned that delft, redware, white salt-glazed stoneware, unrefined stoneware, porcelain, and gray salt-glazed stoneware were the principal ceramic types used by the soldiers, although small quantities of buff-bodied slip-decorated earthenware and brown stoneware were also found. Tobacco pipes were in common use everywhere on Rogers Island, usually with bore diameters of $\frac{4}{64}$ and $\frac{5}{64}$ of an inch and with "R. Tippet" as the most common maker's mark. Fragments of wine bottles were also very common, and we found the largest numbers at the sutler's site near the fort. There were approximately equal numbers of gunflints of French and British origin; we found hundreds of musket balls, most of a size that suggests they were intended to be used in the British Brown Bess musket; and we also found hundreds of small pieces of lead buckshot and birdshot. Lead slag and sprue from casting musket balls were scattered all over the island, and we sometimes found fire-reddened earth marking where the balls had been cast. Some musket balls were flattened from having been fired, others had been chewed and were covered with tooth marks, and still others had been cut or mutilated in various ways.

Ceramics, glass, and armaments were easily the most common artifact categories at this military camp, but there truly was a bit of everything, including spades, axes, buckets, horseshoes, buckles, buttons, knives of several types, two-tined forks, pewter spoons, and even canteens. We did not find some of the more glamorous artifact types that Earl Stott and the Rogers Island Historical Association reportedly found in the 1960s, such as

Jesuit rings, muskets, lead pencils, or Indian beads and trophy skulls, but nevertheless our finds include a wonderful cross section of supplies that the army had brought upriver from Albany.

When Earl Stott first approached me in 1986 with a handful of Spanish and British coins that he had discovered on Rogers Island, I admit that I was surprised. But I should not have been, because from 1991 to 1998 we found well-preserved artifacts everywhere we dug. Among our findings, Jene Romeo has learned in her ongoing zooarcheological research that fresh meat (beef and pork) was quite common and wild animals were not a very significant part of the soldiers' diet. And although fishing was commonly practiced, fish bones have rarely survived in the acidic soil on Rogers Island.

In light of these findings and others, Rogers Island has truly been a rich and fascinating site, not just for its many military and prehistoric artifacts, but for the amazing wealth of information that has made the past come alive for modern visitors to Fort Edward. After all, archeology is not principally about digging or finding objects. Rather, it is asking appropriate questions about the past; followed by the systematic, disciplined recording of information in the field; followed by precise artifact analysis and appropriate conservation; culminating in the publication of all results in a timely and thorough manner. To do less is simply to be a collector or a treasure hunter. I have tried very hard not to overly criticize past digging on Rogers Island in this book, but I would argue that very little "archeology" occurred on Rogers Island prior to 1991.

I am often asked whether we plan any further excavations on Rogers Island, and my answer has been the same since 1998, when we ended our fieldwork. Over an eight-year span, we conducted a very large amount of digging on Rogers Island, arguably too much, and I feel very strongly that it is unethical for archeologists to dig any further if the principal goal becomes "putting on a show for tourists" or adding artifacts to a personal collection. We can justify the removal of an irreplaceable cultural resource only if there are pressing, radically new research questions that cannot be answered any other way. Consequently, I believe that further digging on Rogers Island at this time would be destructive and would serve no legitimate purpose.

Rogers Island is a truly remarkable site, and it needs to be managed and preserved very carefully to ensure that it provides the most information to future generations of scholars. Digging needs to be replaced with interpretation, and the new Rogers Island Visitors Center is starting to tell the story of the soldiers, officers, and Native Americans who once lived on the island (see the box "The Rogers Island Visitors Center"). The story of these early residents and combatants is now being told through drawings and

★ The Rogers Island Visitors Center

The Rogers Island Visitors Center (RIVC) opened on July 6, 2001, having evolved from a Mobil Oil Company terminal building, to a summertime archeology laboratory, to a modern visitors center with the newest exhibits in the region that deal with prehistory and eighteenth-century military history. There are very few centers like it in New York State that contain so much information about archeology. The RIVC has a clear mission, which is to greet visitors to Fort Edward and Washington County, to bring to life the colonial wars in New York State, to tell the story of the Native Americans who *first* settled this land, and to describe the techniques required to conduct archeological and historical research.

The exhibits in the RIVC include hundreds of photographs, hundreds of artifacts, several videotapes featuring local history and archeology, thousands of words, and four life-size "dummies" (a ranger, a Native American, a British regular, and a modern-day archeologist). I might as well admit that my personal favorite among the exhibits is the "archeologist," because he is wearing an old pair of my Herman Survivor boots, my glasses, my felt "Indiana Jones" hat, a khaki shirt from L. L. Bean, and an old pair of dig pants, all of which I had worn on many, many excavations. But what visitors do not know is that minutes before the permanent exhibits opened to the public on July 6, the archeologist was deemed "too flat" in the posterior,

The present appearance of the Rogers Island Visitors Center (RIVC), a far cry from when it was a Mobil Oil Company terminal building!

and Eileen Hannay, manager of the RIVC, was busily stuffing cloth into the rear of his pants to make him a bit more rounded and shapely!

The exhibits tell lively stories; they strive to present the heart and soul of a community, Fort Edward, that has one of the most exciting military pasts in America. The center was designed to complement the historical societies and museums that already existed in the local area, and to encourage visitors to sample other cultural attractions. The average visitor can leave the center and travel to the Fort House Museum, the Washington County Historical Society building, Union Cemetery, the restored Fort Edward train station, the Champlain Canal junction lock, and to historical markers that commemorate events throughout the region. Heritage tourism has become vital to upstate New York, and when visitors leave the RIVC, it is our fervent wish that they will then sample everything else that Fort Edward and Washington County have to offer.

The archeologist "dummy" in the RIVC, dressed to look like archeologist David Starbuck!

The Native American "dummy" in the RIVC, dressed to reflect Native attire in the post-Contact period, after the arrival of European trade goods in the region.

photographs, artifact displays, videotaped presentations, and publications such as this one. Hopefully the joint efforts of archeologists and historians will ensure that the story of the early residents of Fort Edward is told as accurately as possible.

Appendixes

Appendix 1

Artifact Totals for Rogers Island, 1991–1998

Many of the historic artifacts excavated from Rogers Island between 1991 and 1998 are summarized in tables 7.1 and 7.2, whereas the prehistoric artifacts are totaled in chapter 1. In order to convey this information more effectively, appendix 1 uses bar graphs to depict the artifact totals for all major categories of artifacts found on Rogers Island. These categories consist of ceramics, glass, cutlery, sewing equipment, utilitarian artifacts (tools), personal adornments, tobacco pipes, and armaments.

Total Numbers of Ceramic Sherds

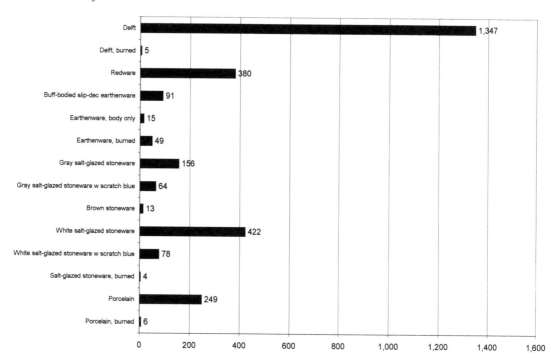

Total Numbers of Glass Fragments

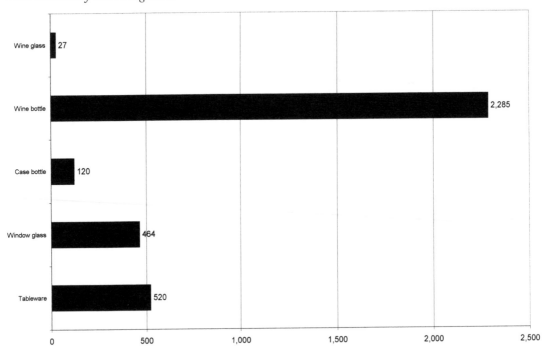

Total Numbers of Cutlery

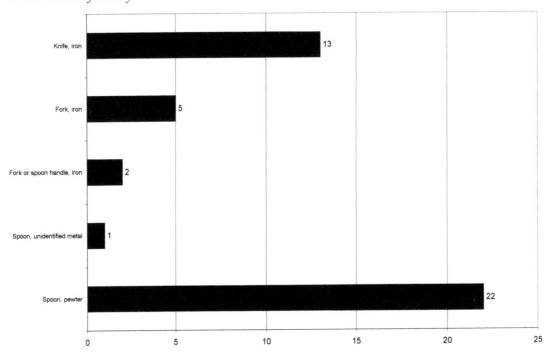

Total Numbers of Sewing Equipment

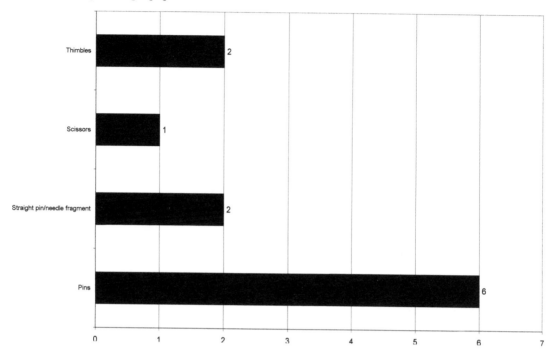

Total Numbers of Utilitarian Items

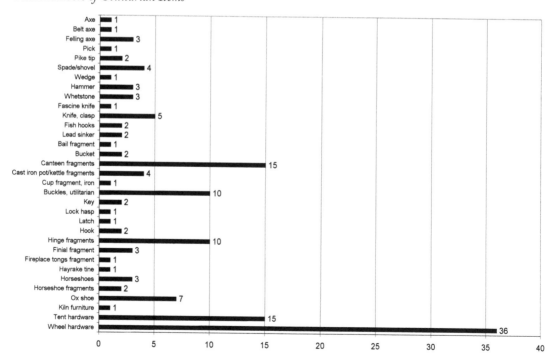

Total Numbers of Personal Adornment Items

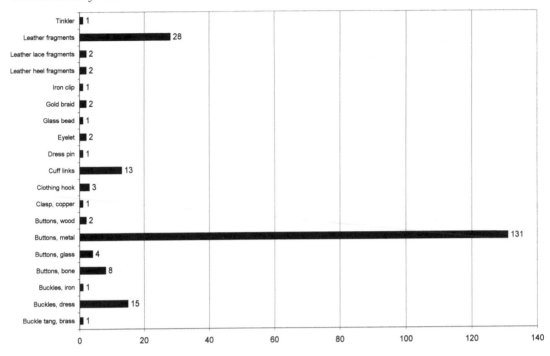

Total Numbers of Tobacco Pipe Fragments

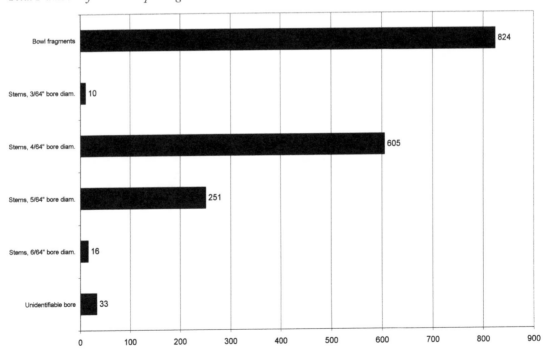

Total Numbers of Coins

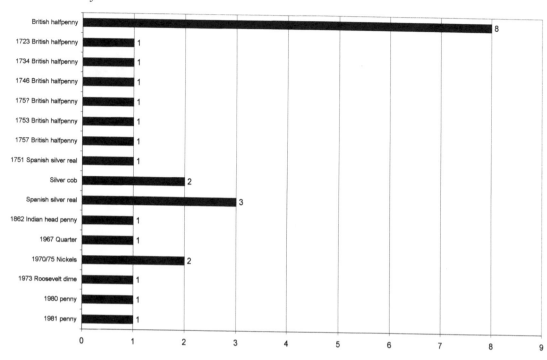

Total Numbers of Armaments

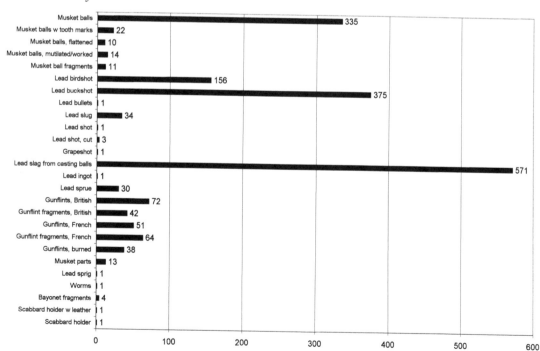

Total Numbers of Medical Supplies

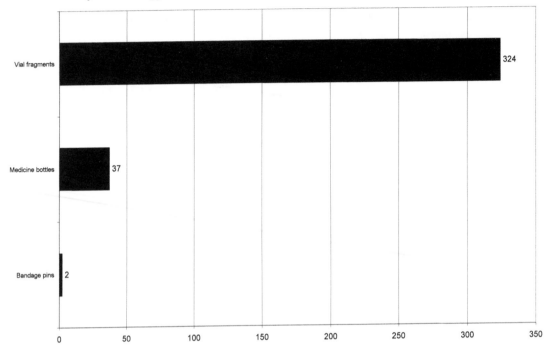

Appendix 2

Ceramics Excavated by Feature on Rogers Island, 1991–1998

Tables 7.1 and 7.2 include the counts of all ceramic sherds as they were excavated from Rogers Island between 1991 and 1998. Appendix 2 uses bar graphs to depict, once again by feature location, these same sherds in order to show the relative proportions of each ceramic type. Those types whose dates of manufacture were clearly later than the French and Indian War (creamware, pearlware, whiteware, and yellowware) have not been included here.

Numbers of Ceramic Sherds, Dwelling 1

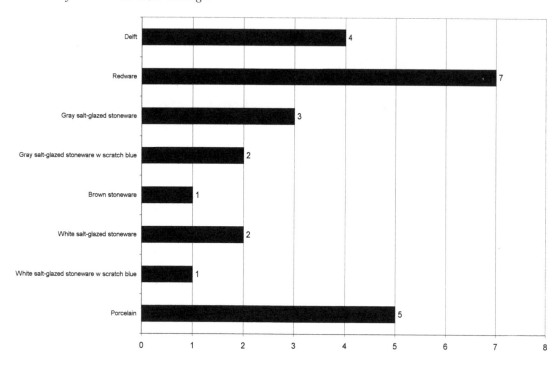

Numbers of Ceramic Sherds, Dwelling 2

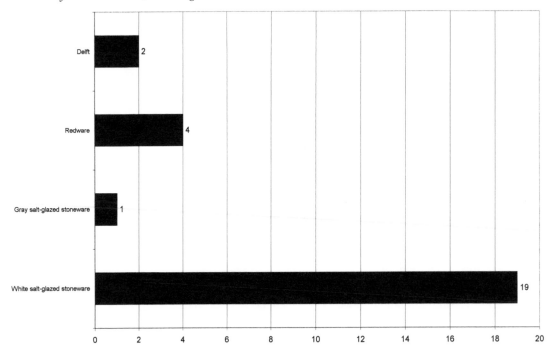

Numbers of Ceramic Sherds, Dwelling 3

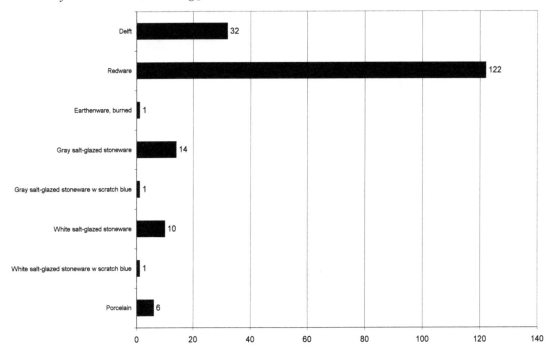

Numbers of Ceramic Sherds, Dwelling 4

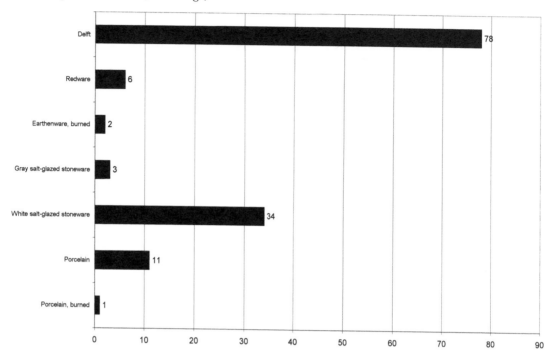

Numbers of Ceramic Sherds, Dwelling 5

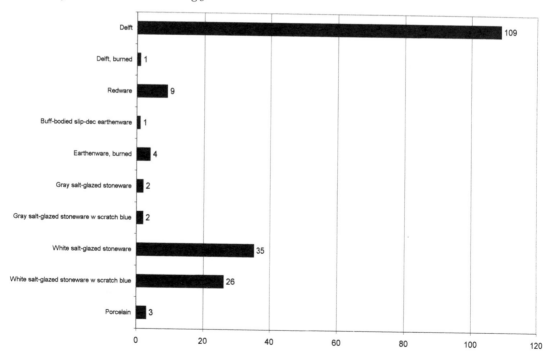

Numbers of Ceramic Sherds, Dwelling 6

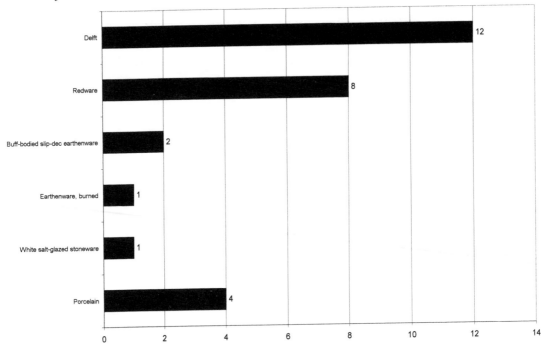

Numbers of Ceramic Sherds, Storehouse

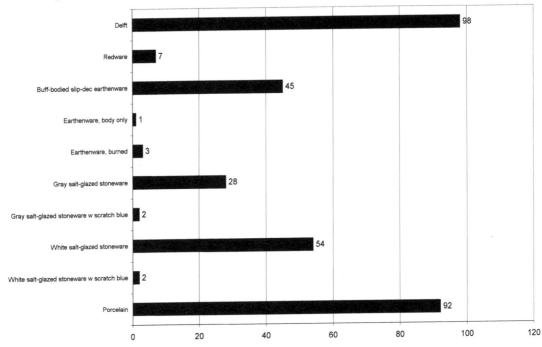

Numbers of Ceramic Sherds, Latrine

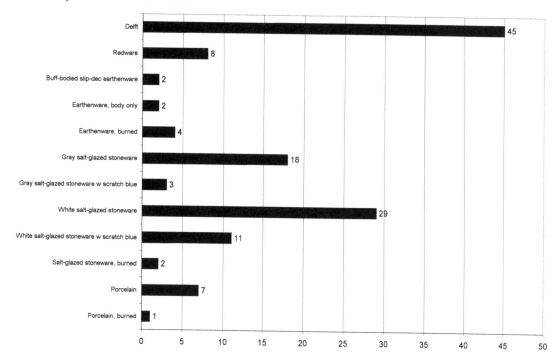

Numbers of Ceramic Sherds, Smallpox Hospital

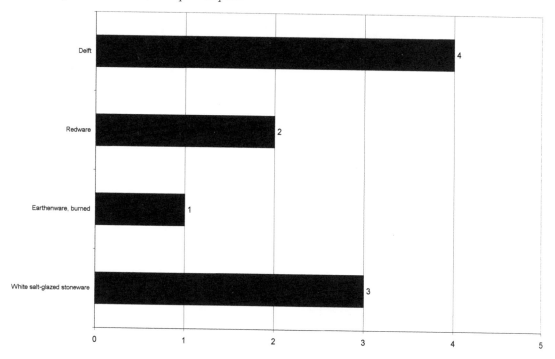

Numbers of Ceramic Sherds, Barracks

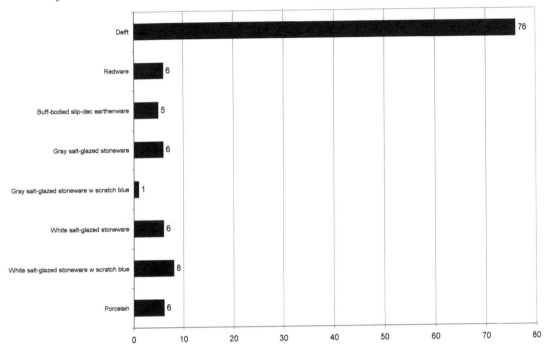

Numbers of Ceramic Sherds, Dump

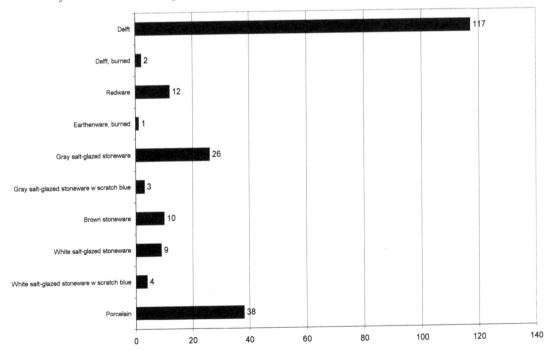

Appendix 3

Tobacco Pipes Excavated by Feature on Rogers Island, 1991–1998

Appendix 3 uses bar graphs to present all fragments of tobacco pipes that were excavated from feature locations on Rogers Island between 1991 and 1998. Stem fragments are displayed according to their bore diameters, and counts of tobacco pipe bowl fragments are also shown. Using this form of presentation, it is immediately apparent that pipes with bores of 4/64 inch were predominant in almost every context on the island, although bores of 5/64 inch were present in significant numbers.

Numbers of Tobacco Pipe Fragments, Dwellings 1–6

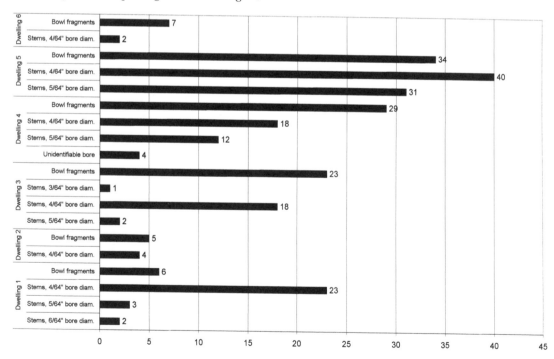

Numbers of Tobacco Pipe Fragments, Other Feature Locations

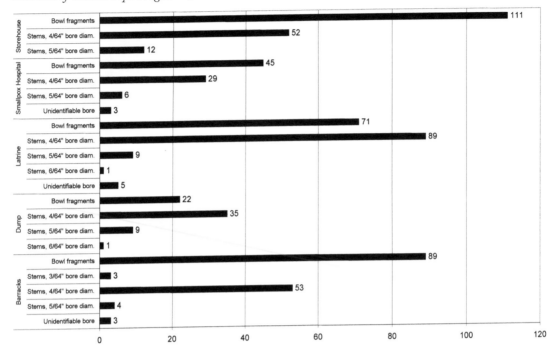

Further Reading

Adler, Winston. "An Island Dig." *Adirondack Life* (July/August 1986): 87–88, 91.

Anderson, Fred. *A People's Army: Massachusetts Soldiers and Society in the Seven Years' War*. Chapel Hill: University of North Carolina Press, 1984.

———. *Crucible of War: The Seven Years' War and the Fate of Empire in British North America, 1754–1766*. New York: Alfred A. Knopf, 2000.

Bougainville, Louis Antoine de. *Adventure in the Wilderness: The American Journals of Louis Antoine de Bougainville, 1756–1760*. Translated and edited by Edward P. Hamilton. Norman: University of Oklahoma Press, 1964.

Brasser, T. J. "Mahican." In *Handbook of North American Indians*, vol. 15. *Northeast*, pp. 198–212. Washington, D.C.: Smithsonian Institution, 1978.

Cooper, James Fenimore. *The Last of the Mohicans*. 1826. Reprint, New York: Penguin Books, 1980.

Cuneo, John R. *Robert Rogers of the Rangers*. Ticonderoga, N.Y.: Fort Ticonderoga Museum, 1988.

Dunn, Shirley W. *The Mohicans and Their Land, 1609–1730*. Fleischmanns, N.Y.: Purple Mountain Press, 1994.

Fitch, Jabez, Jr. *The Diary of Jabez Fitch, Jr., in the French and Indian War, 1757*, 2nd ed. Fort Edward, N.Y.: Rogers Island Historical Association, 1968. Publication no. 1.

Funk, Robert E. "Recent Contributions to Hudson Valley Prehistory." *New York State Museum Memoir*, no. 22. Albany: New York State Museum, 1976.

Gridley, Luke. *Luke Gridley's Diary of 1757 While in Service in the French and Indian War*. Hartford, Conn., 1907.

Grossman, Joel W. *The Excavation, Analysis and Reconstruction of Transitional Period, Late Woodland Period and Colonial Occupations at the Little Wood Creek Site, Fort Edward, Washington County, New York*. Prepared for the Washington County Sewer Authority, Sewer District No. 2, Fort Edward, N.Y., 1990.

Hill, William H. *Old Fort Edward Before 1800*. Fort Edward, N.Y.: Privately printed, 1929.

Loescher, Burt Garfield. *The History of Rogers Rangers*. San Francisco: Printed by the author, 1946.

———. *Rogers Rangers: The First Green Berets*. San Mateo, Calif.: Printed by the author, 1969.

Lossing, Benson J. *The Pictorial Field-Book of the Revolution*. 2 vols. New York: Harper & Brothers, 1851.

Parker, Arthur C. "The Archeological History of New York." *New York State Museum Bulletin*, nos. 235, 236. Albany: The University of the State of New York, 1920.

Parkman, Francis. *Montcalm and Wolfe*. New York: Collier Books, 1962.

Quinn, Paul. "American History for Sale." *Yankee Homes* (June 1988): 21.

Ritchie, William A. *The Archaeology of New York State*. Harrison, N.Y.: Harbor Hill Books, 1980.

Rogers Island Historical Association. *Exploring Rogers Island*, 2nd ed. Fort Edward, N.Y.: Rogers Island Historical Association, 1986.

Snow, Dean R. *The Archaeology of New England*. New York: Academic Press, 1980.

Starbuck, David R. "Anatomy of a Massacre." *Archaeology* 46 (November/December 1993): 42–46.

———. "The Identification of Gender at Northern Military Sites of the Late 18th Century." In *Those of Little Note: Gender, Race, and Class in Historical Archaeology*, ed. Elizabeth Scott, pp. 115–128. Tucson and London: University of Arizona Press, 1994.

———. "The Rogers Island Archaeological Site: Transforming Myths into Strategies for Interpreting and Managing a Major Encampment from the French and Indian War." In *Cultural Resource Management*, ed. Jordan E. Kerber, pp. 243–260. Westport, Conn.: Bergin & Garvey, 1994.

———. "Four Years of Archaeological Research on Rogers Island, an Encampment of the French and Indian War." *Journal of Middle Atlantic Archaeology* 12 (1996): 149–161.

———. "America's Forgotten War." *Archaeology* 50 (January/February 1997): 60–63.

———. "Military Hospitals on the Frontier of Colonial America." *Expedition* 39, 1 (1997): 33–45. University of Pennsylvania.

———. *The Great Warpath*. Hanover, N.H.: University Press of New England, 1999.

———. "Military Archaeology of America's Colonial Wars." In *Old and New Worlds*, ed. Geoff Egan and R. L. Michael, pp. 195–202. Oxford: Oxbow Books, 1999.

———. *Massacre at Fort William Henry*. Hanover, N.H.: University Press of New England, 2002.

———, ed. *Archeology in Fort Edward*. Queensbury, N.Y.: Adirondack Community College, 1995.

Steele, Ian K. *Betrayals: Fort William Henry & the "Massacre."* New York: Oxford University Press, 1990.

Todish, Timothy J. *America's First First World War: The French & Indian War, 1754–1763*. Ogden, Utah: Eagle's View Publishing Company, 1988.

———. "Rangers at Fort Edward." *Muzzleloader* (July/August 1990): 54–58.

———. *The Annotated and Illustrated Journals of Major Robert Rogers*. Fleischmanns, N.Y.: Purple Mountain Press, 2002.

United States Army. *Ranger Handbook*. Fort Benning, Ga.: Ranger Training Brigade, United States Army Infantry School, July 1992.

Woods, Lynn. "A History in Fragments." *Adirondack Life* 25, 7 (1994): 30–37, 61, 68–71, 78–79.

Zaboly, Gary S. "A Lodging for the Night: A Brief Study of Some Types of Wilderness Shelters Used During the French and Indian War." *Muzzleloader* (March/April 1989): 47–51.